Monsters
&
Madmen
A Death Row Experiment

NICK YARRIS

Monsters & Madmen
A Death Row Experiment

Revised Edition
10 9 8 7 6 5 4 3 2

www.escarpmentpress.weebly.com
INDIAN LAND, SC

Front Cover Image © Shutterstock Image #351854759
Fierce Gargoyle-Fantasy Winged Beast
draco77vector

Dedication

I dedicate this work to Harriet "Jayne" Yarris. It was you who inspired me to find whatever that is good and decent about myself. You stuck by me, "Sport," and that meant the world of difference to me while I was going through my bleakest of times. I will never let go of my vow to you to always be a nice man. The rest, I see now, is just my being part of life with dignity. It is up to me to put into perspective who I am in that context.

Contents

Acknowledgments

I would like to acknowledge my younger self for having the poise and dignity within to find the courage to rise above my situation.

I go around the world praising others who develop well, regardless of what they had to face in life. I should then acknowledge my own advancements in life just as unabashedly as I give praise in this way.

So to you, young Nick Yarris, I thank you for allowing me the chance to use the time spent while in prison to now have a purpose in sharing my life with so many humans today.

Preface

I first learned of Nick Yarris when I viewed the Netflix documentary, *The Fear of 13*, which was subsequently followed by the release of his best-selling book with the same title. To say I was touched by his story would be an understatement.

Curious, I surfed the Internet until I found the listing for the book on Amazon.com. It was published by Random House. However, I also discovered that *Monsters & Madmen*, was one of three books that Nick subsequently self-published after *The Fear of 13* was published by Random House. I took a peek inside the self-published books and saw that they were in need of some significant formatting and editing. With that in mind, I tracked Nick down on Facebook and sent him a message, offering to correct those issues for "one of the books" at no charge to him. I felt compelled to do something for this man who had suffered so much at the hands of the penal system. I fully expected to not hear back, but, hey, I figured it was worth a try.

To my surprise, several days later, I received a response from Nick, thanking me for my offer and offering to share in any future royalties that a revised edition of *Monsters & Madmen* might generate. I declined the royalties, but, after some gentle arm twisting on my part reached an agreement with Nick for me to re-format, edit, and publish his book under my imprint.

And so it began.

In working on Nick's manuscript, I learned that he has been married four times. Three of those marriages ended in divorce. In the book, however, he only refers to wife number two, Jacque Schaffer, (from whom he was divorced while still incarcerated), and Laura Ann Yarris (to whom he is happily married, and to whom this book is dedicated). But, nowhere in the manuscript was there any mention of how he met either spouse, or under what condition their relationships came to fruition. So, I asked Nick to please describe for me how each marriage came about. Here is what he wrote:

"I met Jacque Schaffer in 1987, when she came to Huntingdon prison to visit death row inmates who were seeking outside help regarding the living conditions . . . within the housing units. Jacque was a member of the Pennsylvania Prison Society whose members were seeking to end solitary confinement. Initially she wanted to know why I was not complaining about my situation, and why I had no complaints about the torture and harsh conditions in the most notorious prison in Pennsylvania.

"In the months following my meeting Jacque, I became the very first man in America to seek DNA testing to prove my innocence. It was . . . this act, of trying to prove through science that I was innocent of rape and murder that made Jacque and I bond. We fell in love during the years that my appeals for DNA testing were going on. We had a cheaply staged marriage in the maximum security unit visiting room, during the entire marriage, I only had non-contact visits with her . . . sitting apart from one another, and viewing one another through security glass.

"As austere as the arrangement was, I really had a fully developed marriage with all of the trappings, except for the physical aspects, which we were denied. For many years, I honestly felt that as long as I had this person outside who truly believed in me, I could endure much of what was done to me on the inside of prison. I had this person who wrote letters and helped with the burden my mother had borne for many years of trying to get help or attention for me.

"I hated the way time stole our dreams, and each time the courts let me down without allowing me DNA testing, how my being married made me feel guilty for the time of her life that Jacque was losing. All I know about being able to talk to a woman, how to behave as I think a man should, all really came from Jacque.

"During the many hours we spent in visits, what we had was unique, something only a few people in life have had the opportunity to appreciate. I got to live out a love affair by day, while at night I lived within a soul-chewing, horror show of the prison that was Huntingdon. I had to step away from the most unpleasant world you could imagine, come into the light of hopeful dreams and loving words, only to have that be cast aside once Jacque left the visiting room. It was a doomed relationship.

"I met my current wife, Laura Ann Yarris, in 2016. I had just returned to the U.K. to attempt to fix things in my life. Before then, I was actually homeless and living on the streets of Los Angeles. Since gaining my freedom in 2004, I had wasted my time on two bad relationships, and *whatever money I had was gone, along with both women who had wasted so much of my life post-release.*

"What led to my meeting Laura was a documentary film comprised of] an interview I gave, entitled 'The Fear of 13. That film was released on a number of movie platforms and was hugely popular. A publisher in the UK offered to re-format and re-print my first book, formerly titled '7 Days to Live,' with a new title, based on the title of the documentary. For me, It was a chance to get out of being on the streets, and living in a motor home with my two dogs, which was really a low time for me.

"It has often been said that happenstance, being in the right place at the right time, is how people meet in life. Laura and I met in a restaurant on the side of the 303 Motorway in Basingstoke, England. That's it! No big romantic swooning, with a courtship and dates. It was like we just knew we were going to be together. All I know is that somehow, some way, I wanted to stay with her and heal. I wanted to feel better about myself and find someone who was worthy of my time and love, after being on a downturn for a while.

"It was my telling Laura about my offer from this UK publisher that led to my deciding to finally write 'Monsters & Madmen.' What a relief to have someone so into my writing and work as an artist that they wanted to know more of what I had never shared. I thought that if others knew what I had gone through in that Pittsburgh prison for three years, maybe they would appreciate what drives me. Moreover, I felt that I was finally free to tell things about my prison ordeal in my way. So, in the best

humor, and with all the gusto I could muster, I let fly with this amazing story.

"Laura and I are going strong, and my writing is as important to her now as it was when we first met. We seemingly got it right, and her daughters, Bethany and Zara, complete the family we have together.

"Writing this book was a treat for me, as I had never written a work just to please my lover. I seriously just sat alone for several days and let rip this tale, knowing that it was really only meant as a gift to one person in the whole equation, my then wife to be, Laura."

I think just reading what Nick has written about his two wives should convince the reader of the sincerity of what follows: "Monsters & Madmen."

Joe Perrone Jr.
Escarpment Press, 2020

1

"No way are we letting *these* men out of their cells!"

Pittsburgh Penitentiary, January 1995

In 1993, Pennsylvania opened SCI Greene, which is a supermax prison located in the westernmost part of the Keystone State, in Greene County, some sixty miles Southwest of Pittsburgh. Officially it is known as State Correctional Institution Greene. It is totally isolated.

Within two years of opening its main housing units to general-population prisoners, the new "supermax" unit located within the prison would become one of two central Death Row units used by the state.

At the time, 225 men were under sentence of death in Pennsylvania's penal system. The majority of the men expected to go to SCI Greene were those men who came from Huntingdon Prison, located in Central Pennsylvania. This ancient relic in the system had just been ordered by the federal courts to transfer 154 men housed there on Death Row out of there and into SCI Greene.

At some point, the Pennsylvania Department of Corrections had to decide which inmates were to be housed at which prison, both for reasons of security and practicality. The courts also mandated that the outdated system of twenty-three hours a day of solitary confinement needed to be stopped, and that men sentenced to die deserved to be out of their cells more.

It is early afternoon. The story begins within an enclosed setting located inside of the interior of a brand new, specially designed "PSYCHIATRIC DEATH ROW UNIT," perched high atop the main prison buildings within the penitentiary compound itself. It is a unit made initially for punishment and administrative segregation of prisoners who were violent or in need of protection. The building is odd – three stories high – yet split on five levels (with the uppermost part surrounded by heavy wire). It is intimidating.

The only way in or out of the top level is a slow elevator connecting the unit to the ground floor. Once inside of this rickety box, which is about five feet squared, you feel trapped within it. It is all part of a unit that is a hell hole all of its own design.

The new unit in Greene County has day rooms and recreational areas set up to allow controlled times of up to eight hours per day for death row men to be let out of their cells.

While the usual concerns of separating inmates who have testified against fellow death row prisoners mandates that a lot of the decision to transfer men is security related, it applies only to a small group. However, there came a point where the administration balked at the "monsters and madmen" they held being allowed out of their cells.

The idea of serial killers with convictions for killing numerous victims being allowed out of their cells to interact with the mentally weak was scary. What about the cannibals who became even more aggressive after years of torment from fellow inmates? Then there was the question of what to do with men who had assaulted staff, raped other inmates in the past, or were on heavy medications to curb their psychosis?

No, there had to be some place truly isolated for the worst case men to be held while Pennsylvania tried to comply with the courts. No way could Pennsylvania risk serious incidents in a new prison that was meant to be a very new statement about Pennsylvania and its modern penology. An idea was then put forth to segregate the "worst of the worst" in the old Pittsburgh Penitentiary.

There, in a sealed unit that was inaccessible to the main prison, they would begin the first ever "Psychiatric Death Row" unit. There were forty-two cells and two "Death Watch" cells set up in Pittsburgh for what would soon be the setting for this experiment. The State was claiming that the forty-eight men whom they picked out could be held back from the court's orders because they were all too deranged to act accordingly.

Now, for whatever reason there was, with forty-eight new Death Row men being transferred to Pittsburgh prison, there had to be a selection of the staff who would be running the unit. This factor, more than any other, led to a lot of madness afterward. The men working there were told going in that they would be in charge of forty-eight mentally ill, violently deranged Death Row prisoners. Having guards, who were the least equipped mentally to handle the unit, is what led to a complete breakdown of control.

The average prison guard working in that unit had numerous infractions or complaints filed against them for abuse by prisoners. They were used in this disciplinary housing setting because of their ability to conduct brutal reprisals against inmates who acted out. They were thugs with clubs, who had no compunction or hesitation to inflict pain; these men were not trained to deal with psychosis.

They were also not given extensive training in the understanding of mental illness. They were in no way equipped to handle men meant to be in a psychiatric hospital, and they treated all forty-eight men as if they were in need of punishment.

When one combines the worst of the worst prisoners condemned to die, together with the deeply disturbed minds of prison guards, who have shown a propensity for violence, the outcome would, of course, be chaos.

In 1995, no one conducted psych tests on the staff of the new unit inside the prison to see how they would react to being around a man who could laugh in their faces about how he had butchered a disabled child. No one took the time to evaluate the men who would have to be around a man who had tortured women and was racially driven. The administration used guards from the "hole" (or punishment setting) to then treat mentally disturbed men. No one considered conducting a "Princeton Experiment," because one had not yet been tried or even conceived.

So, how did I end up being able to tell you this story? Let's just say that I was deemed to be one of the most likely Death Row prisoners housed in Pennsylvania in 1995 to be sent to a nuthouse like that. I fit all of the criteria. With violence on my record, convicted of a psychologically based murder, and having escaped Death Row briefly in 1985, it was a "no-brainer" decision that I was sent there.

The day that all forty-eight men were placed on a prison security bus to be transferred out of Huntingdon prison (where I had just spent the previous twelve years being locked up) was personally eerie for me.

On the way *into* Huntingdon in 1983, I was the only Death Row man on a bus full of prisoners. There were only twenty-seven men in the whole state of Pennsylvania sentenced to die at that time. As I left that day in 1995, I was a middle-aged man, witnessing my own growth, from when I first landed there, to when they finally shut that place down. I felt sad that I would lose all of my comforts and the ability to have a set routine. I had no clue what was waiting for me next, while I had three men on the bus who had tried previously to murder me. To sit with your arms and legs restrained for hours on a bus with men known for their ability to get out of their restraints to kill or maim was a marathon exercise in preparing for an attack.

I was also wearing a fifty-thousand volt electrical charge that was strapped to my kidneys with a thick leather belt, because I was a former escapee. So, I also had to deal with what would happen if anything kicked it off and I was electrocuted. It would be horrific if I were zapped by the guard holding the remote-controlled activator of my restraint due to a fight. I sat quietly and kept myself alert to things, and each man seemed so muted and scared of what was waiting for us all at the end of this ride, that no one spoke the whole way.

Once the bus had fully stopped inside the walls of Pittsburgh Penitentiary, the guards surrounded it, and there was dead silence for a long period.

There must have been twenty-five or more prison guards, all of whom were in heavy gear. They started taking one man at a time, sandwiched between two guards, and marching them off of the bus and into the new unit, in which they would now be housed.

I was glad that, unlike during my very first bus ride to Death Row, I did not get a beating, nor was I thrown into a cell. This time, I was part of a group of men being taken inside, and I was no bother to anyone at first. Within forty minutes of the bus pulling up to the gates of Pittsburgh, each of the forty-eight men had every nook and cranny of his body searched before he was put into a cell.

Now I want to go back to the frame of mind that I needed to have back then to survive. I'd like to take you with me through my ordeal in a way that will give some perspective to how I was driven through it all.

Until now, I deliberately did *not* want to share this story, due to the personal pain it causes me even now. It's hard to believe that, after I have told so much of the story of my life previously, this one segment of time has made it so difficult for me to relate my development. Previously, I have tried to just write it all off as a waste of time. I guess that just goes to show me once more that everything happens for a reason, and that, in time, what we hold onto fiercely will change later as well.

So here is my story, from day one of my entry, when I was labeled one of the "Monsters and Madmen," and subjected to this pitiful experiment . . .

I am standing in a prison cell that is made of cinder blocks that are painted light blue. Facing me is a sliding metal door, painted gray, which has a flap cut into it, called a "pie hole," which is about twenty-four inches long, and about six inches high. It's at about waist high level on the door. There is an additional cut in the door about four inches wide, by twenty-two inches high (mesh screens cover both openings). This is to allow staff to see into and speak to prisoners without the "pie hole" being open. These openings are designed so the door to your cell never cuts off sound or air flow. It is also through these upright cuts in the doors that you can see outside of your cell to the surrounding cell area nearby.

I am wearing only an orange jumpsuit, a thin white T-shirt, white boxers shorts, blue, canvas prison-issued shoes with white rubber soles, and brown socks. The two, upright cuts in each cell door have heavy metal wire, crisscrossed in diamond patterns. The outside surface area has a weird pattern that your eyes need to adjust to in order to make sense of what you are seeing. At least one of your eyes has to look past metal wire to focus, and I find it annoying to have to do this while wearing corrective eye glasses

I look to my right, and see that bolted on the wall inside of my cell is a metal speaker cover for the intercom/ speaker/microphone. This how the guard, located inside a glass control booth in the hallway outside, will talk to me. Through the control booth windows, I can see a single guard standing inside. I will speak to that officer while I am locked inside my six foot wide by eight foot long cell.

Inside my cell to the right is a metal toilet that has a sink with taps fitted atop it that is all made out of metal — a solid unit that is securely bolted to the wall. Above the sink is an eight by twelve inch metal plate, meant to serve as a mirror. You'll have to get used to the blurred "you" reflecting back at you whenever you shave. That's all that is available.

Behind me on the wall to my left is a metal bunk with a four-inch thick plastic mattress on top of it. There is a plastic pillow on it as well. At some point, a set of sheets and towels will be given to me. Along the other wall, opposite the bed, is a simple metal table with a single metal chair that has been welded to its base. The desk and flat table back are bolted to the wall as well. There are two metal hooks for my towels, or to hang clothes on, opposite the toilet at shoulder level by my door.

Along the back wall are two windows. *Don't bother*, I tell myself. *You've already checked them out. Cannot see shit!*

The wire, screen mesh outside is so thick over the glass that, combined with the metal screens built into the window frame from the inside of the glass, it's all but impossible to see much. It's like an image from a science fiction movie, where they replicate the inside of a fly's eye. You really have to see the skyline of a city through this metal mesh to appreciate what it's like. It's a waste of fucking time looking outside, because you'll only get a headache trying to see anything.

Looking out of my cell through one of the upright cuts in the metal door, I can see I am in a squared pod of cells. They are mostly made of the same cinder blocks and wire mesh, and all painted the same robin's egg blue as my cell. There are seven other cells in my pod, and one semi-open area with a plastic curtain hung across it. A set of metal bars can be slid across the opening. This is the "shower room." The bars are set up to seal it like a cell, and can be remotely opened from within from the control room. I can see that this must serve as the shower room for all of the men on the lone pod, with whom I shared cells.

In the center of the pod is a caged area with a shiny metal picnic table bolted to the floor, surrounded by four metal seats also bolted to the floor. This is the day room.

There is a gray metal door sealing this area off from the cells, through which men can be let in.   In the corner of this cage is a blue plastic phone bolted to the day-room wire mesh wall off in a corner.

Outside of the mesh day-room is a metal door on either end of the pod allowing the guards to enter from the door right next to the shower to my left, or from the other end of the last cell, which is to my right. My cell is right in the middle of the pod, so I can see all but the two corner cells to my left or right. I can clearly see who is in the other cells, if the men stand at their door.

It is not like I have to stand at my door to be heard. With each pod of cells only spread about twenty-five feet apart, you feel like you are in a connected unit where each man can join in your conversation instantly.   You're limited in your ability to blot out the others only by a set of headphones or sleep. Otherwise, it's very up close and personal. You share each sneeze and every cough, and nearly every word is free game.

That lone telephone bolted to the wall in the day room is your only instant communication to the outside. It is on this lone line of communication that all eight men on the pod call the outside world via collect calls.   All calls are recorded and listened to by the staff.

This pod, called "C" Pod, is now my home. It is one of three pods that face the north side of this building. In the center section, between the north and south sides of the unit, is a laughable area called the "outside exercise area." Out there, four cages are set up that are five feet wide and twelve feet long, literally long enough to do a silly jog that ends each way with a short turn to come back. Basically, they are four dog kennels wrapped in so much wire that you literally cannot see direct sunlight on a sunny day.

No one got onto the top floor unless the guards at the top allow the elevator to come up there by use of security keys. There is only one way in and one way out except for stairs attached to the outside, which are always locked.

I had just come up on this creaking, horribly slow and shaky elevator, and two enormous prison officers were crowding me against the back wall, using their clubs to hold me against the wall. The whole thing was so small that I soon felt on the cusp of feeling smothered inside of a five foot by five foot, squared box.

When I walked to my pod on the arms of my escorts, I was first stopped by the administration waiting there. There were about twelve in all. We referred to them as "White Shirts and Shot-callers." They were the folks who decided where, when, and what you got.

Right in front of the guards who were holding me, they read aloud what I was convicted of, when I was sentenced to die, and then into which pod these guards were to take me. It was right at that point that I learned that I was under psychiatric care, because I was deemed too mentally disturbed to be sent to SCI-Greene County prison. I was informed on the spot that, due the violence I had previously exhibited inside prison, (and how I was convicted of a mentally deranged crime), I was unfit to be trusted out of my cell.

Furthermore, due to my previous escape, I was also a risk to the orderly function of a normal Death Row unit. I was offered medications then, and the whole time I stood there in mute silence.

The staff concluded my "welcome" to the unit by informing me that as I was now under psychiatric detention. Also, I was now also subject to the rules and regulations of the mental health division. I had no clue what any of that meant at first. I just had a floor filled with male and female staff hear it announced what a mentally fucked up person I was, and how, since I was deemed such a nutcase, I was not to be trusted in an open setting. My focus was held by the fly on the wall behind them that I envisioned myself to be.

When you have something so ugly hanging over you, you do not quip one line jokes. You own the humiliation of the moment, whether guilty or not, because you are being held up to the light that no one seems to handle. It sucked.

As I was taken out of my chains and forced to strip down naked one last time to be searched before I was finally put into my cell, I knew that each man who was to fill one of the other cells would be put through the same routine as well. I bet that each one would feel just as shitty as I did.

I didn't know it at the time, while I focused on all of that initiation process, but each man who was brought into my pod after me, I soon learned, was being set up to be part of one of the sickest experiments ever imagined.

The guards who would be assigned to this unit were led by a staff sergeant. Unfortunately for us all, he was a "rage-aholic" of a man, whose diminutive stature of only five feet, six inches tall, was mated to a huge ego. His level of outbursts and uncontrolled venomous acts would be on display right away to all who slighted him.

My first confrontation with the man who ran day-to-day operations on all six pods was ugly. He stood in front of my cell and read aloud the newspaper accounts of my case that he had printed out on white sheets of paper. His version of my incarceration was punctuated with lots of nasty comments, but, for the record, here is what he made sure he let me know that he knew about me. His "story" went like this:

Linda Mae Craig was working in the Tri-State Mall located in the state of Delaware back in December of 1981. As she left work at 4:00 p.m. on December 15, 1981, police said that I ran or walked up to her and punched her in the face as she got into her car, thus breaking her teeth. They said I then dragged her out of her shoes (which were found there the next morning where her car was). They said I put Mrs. Craig into her own car, and then drove away with her into Pennsylvania, located only some three miles away.

Police said that I then cut away Mrs. Craig's clothes with a knife, and that I raped her. The police claimed I stabbed Mrs. Craig brutally six times in the chest with the same knife, and that I dumped her dying body in the parking lot of a church where the rape took place.

Police said that I then drove Mrs. Craig's own car right past her home and left it along the side of the road near her house with the engine running, car doors locked , along with the interior lights left on inside . . . The authorities claimed I "staged the interior of the car," complete with my leaving behind the bloody gloves worn during the crime, as a taunt to the police upon finding this all.

My presenter then went on to highlight my escape in 1985, along with all of the infractions on my record within the department of corrections. It was all summed up nicely when he leaned forward and told me how much "fuckin' fun he was going to have with a sick piece of shit like me." That was five minutes after I was placed into my cell.

What made me "special" to this man was that the authorities said that I did my crimes because I was mentally sick and twisted. They said that I had stalked Mrs. Craig for weeks, and that I planned her murder in a psychotically driven scheme.

The authorities said that because I was deranged and on drugs (and that I had a mentally malfunctioning brain anyway), that I killed Mrs. Craig because I had a girlfriend of three weeks break my heart. Reading all of this to me caused my pal to laugh aloud.

The fact that I had blood that was B-positive, which was the same as that found in evidence at the scene of the crime, all made it that much easier to convict me. In his mind, it was also a valid reason for this man to mock me.

My life in prison, before this man entered it, had been brutal enough, but now I was being reminded all over of what a piece of shit I was in his eyes, and how he was going to use that information to hurt me further.

I was sent to Death Row after a fast, three-day long murder trial. Then, in 1982, following only four hours of deliberation, the jury decided my punishment. I was sentenced to die in the state's electric chair. I was 21 years old.

I was angry, and people were constantly taking shots at me inside of jail, physically. I went to my first state prison and assaulted an officer during a fight with another inmate only two months into my stay there. That assault was used by the governor, (along with an escape attempt in 1981 by another Death Row inmate named John Lesko, which had nothing to do with me), to then lock down every prisoner in solitary confinement in Pennsylvania. I was so hated by every man who blamed me for them being in solitary confinement, that I was initially shunned by all who occupied cells around me on Death Row.

Sgt. "Rage" made it clear that I was there before him to now answer for all of my misdeeds like those, and for any others that he could think of. Because I really did not like that I was now in a sealed unit with a man who could do virtually anything he wished to me, so I kept quiet throughout his whole performance.

As I stood before that door listening to him belittle me, I had a total of one hundred and five years on top of my actual sentence of death, so I was never meant to *ever* get out alive. If I was not executed, the number of years to be served by me would be fatal anyway. That man knew this and so did I at the time. All he had to do was point it out to me rudely to make me feel as low as possible. Never in his wildest dreams could he have ever imagined I would get out one day and tell this story.

There was one other prisoner already on this new pod of mine when I was put into my cell. I could not see him, but I saw a shadow moving inside of the cell when he would walk toward his door. I waited silently for what was to come next.

Having this faceless man listen to my history and having the same thing probably done to him by the sergeant made neither one of us want to speak. I learned that it was bad form to be the first one to speak when put into a new setting anyway. But this was some new shit I had never faced before. This guy was making a point of playing with each guy coming into the pod, or maybe I was just one of the few whom he was going to toy with. Either way, it really did not matter, because I was screwed.

When you are placed under the control of someone who is mentally disturbed, it makes you feel fearful and alone, and gives you a sense of vulnerability to know you are on a "list." It is daunting to think that this guy has so much power that he can let three guys out of their cells in the day room who are all armed. If they choose to attack you, you are done. He can push one button from the control booth to open a cell and your life is over.

I knew from that first moment that I had to tread very carefully with this man.

2

Every Kind of Crazy

Ten minutes after I was put into my new cell, I heard all the sounds of the guards bringing in a new guy to the pod. In short order, the sliding metal and glass doors leading to the outside hallway popped open. From my cell-door crack I saw bodies moving as they walked our way, past the central control unit. I stood at my door watching as the door slid open to the pod. Then two officers brought in the next man. "Damn" I said under my breath, "not *him* . . ."

The very first guy I was going to have to be with on my pod was none other than Roland. (I am loath to be sharing this creature's tale at all.) He stood about five feet eight *maybe* on a good day of his life, and weighed about 135 pounds to 140 pounds? Yeah, that was about right. Roland was a black guy who had a shaved head and spoke with a lisp. He had a medium-colored complexion. His voice was somewhere between effeminate and menacing. He was a chameleon. This dude was so good at fooling people that I always had to remember who he was—*and* what our personal history was.

There had always been hate between us.

Now, the rules were simple on Death Row: If you wanted everyone to leave you alone, you dealt with your enemies yourself. If you tipped off the guards, or let them know that you had someone after you, everyone lined up together and got your ass back for being a "rat." So, hate him or not, that sicko was my new housemate of sorts. I would have to be very careful with him being so close by, without saying a word to anyone about our feud.

Who was Roland? Sergeant Rage made a real fuss about telling us all about him when the guards got him into his cell. According to him, these were the facts:

Roland was living in Pittsburgh at the time of his arrest in the late 1980s for minor felony crimes. His path to Death Row was as sick as anyone could have imagined. In 1988, Roland kidnapped three women in their late eighties, and beat them to death with his bare hands. His nickname in the newspaper was "The Karate Killer."

Yes, that lame, evil, and twisted psycho had been in jail and learned martial arts early on. He then got out of jail, only to later on use this attacking style of self defense on his victims. A lot of what happened has been pretty much kept from the newspapers, or is not widely known outside of law books and prison records.

Unfortunately for Roland, though, Sergeant Rage was working there in Pittsburgh when it all took place. Roland was in custody and serving time for a series of crimes — mostly burglary, or robbery — that had him in the local Pittsburgh county jail located about five miles from the state prison. He was locked up in a place called the Washington County Jail awaiting trial. While he was there, an inmate escaped from custody and badly embarrassed the authorities. Roland used this incident as a ploy to get himself out of jail.

Roland was able to completely immerse himself in anything that he said about himself, so he went to the authorities claiming that he could help the FBI find a local escapee named William Wallace. Believe it or not, the FBI went right along with it.

Sergeant Rage was shocked that Roland somehow had used his maniacal charms to convince some dimwit FBI agent that if they let him out of jail, he could go and find Wallace.

Roland was in no way not going to take this opportunity at freedom, and pretended that he himself was an FBI agent. He put on a suit and tie, and began going around Pittsburgh trying to catch the man whose location he had claimed to know.

At first, he robbed local, small time drug dealers, all the while claiming he was an FBI agent. He beat a young woman with a bottle in front of her three-year-old child when she "refused" to give up the information which he sought from her about William Wallace. The woman didn't even know a man named Wallace, and had only met Roland at a bus stop in the area ten minutes before he savagely beat her.

But all of this hunting for someone he probably did not even know soon became boring for Roland, and he grew tired of looking for someone with no chance of actually finding him. Since he didn't have a car, he tried to abduct a woman in her forties, who was sitting alone in a parking lot. Roland tried to convince her that someone had messed with her tire, but she was able deflect his attempt to do anything to her, and went to the police to report the incident soon afterward.

An hour after he attempted to abduct the first woman, Roland went up to an eighty-eight-year-old lady who was just getting into her car at a mall. He conned her into thinking she had trouble with her car's rear tire, just as he had done earlier with the younger woman. He got the old woman into her car by convincing her that he was going to care of whatever was broken. He got behind the wheel and drove her over to another part of the big parking lot area of the mall. It was there that he also picked up two of the woman's elderly friends who had been at lunch with her, and conned them into joining them in the car. They all went passively along with Roland, and they drove off, eventually stopping in some woods nearby in an area located just outside of Pittsburgh.

Roland got them out of the car, one by one, standing them up against some trees, and then beat all three of them to death with his bare hands. He made sport of his victims, breaking each of the three women's legs first. He made sure that none of them could escape his terror. He delighted in making them suffer, going to work on them with spinning kicks, or karate blows to their necks and faces. He practiced his elbow blows on one woman's face eleven times. He took trinkets from each victim as he beat on them, ripping earrings out while stomping one victim to death. He shattered one woman's hip while standing on her, and danced about in joy on as if he were on a trampoline . . .

This unbelievably horrific crime was one of the worst examples of the FBI allowing a man out of jail only to have him commit murders. To the Bureau, it was all a bad nightmare, one they wished they could be over, so they could forget it. This was why it never received national attention in America's news. It was why Sergeant Rage felt that Roland needed badly to die for his crimes.

I cringed as Sergeant Rage went on and on about Roland. He concentrated on what a low individual Roland was for some of the twisted acts he had performed, as he continued to read us the details.

In what was described by the coroner as a "prolonged effort to inflict as much pain as possible on the victims" those three, poor old ladies were subjected to the sickest imaginable deaths anyone could conjure up. They said it took an hour for Roland Roland to beat all three old women to death, only because he made so much sport of it. He harmed them just enough to still allow them to crawl on the ground in a feeble attempt to flee, all the while as he sat on them and laughed.

He mocked them as they pleaded for their lives, too, all as he finished them off one at a time, until he had slowly murdered all three in the most pitiless way he could.

For Sergeant Rage, this was a particularly nasty moment, but he cheered up a bit as he pointed out how the jury was so angry and wanted the nightmare to be over as fast as humanly possible, so it convicted Roland of first degree murder in just twenty minutes.

Now I know from experience that it usually takes about fifteen minutes just to sign the fully completed set of verdict slips, a process in which the jurors are asked to write their names on sheets of paper next each count the man who is on trial is facing. So, basically, what that meant was that Roland was convicted the moment he sat his sick ass in the defendant's chair at the start of the trial.

On the day of the crime, what Roland did after using all sorts of dirty tricks to break those woman's limbs and bodies was not even *close* to showing how truly sick he was. (Even today, it blows my mind every time I think of Sergeant Rage describing it all.)

You see, directly after killing those three old ladies, like a savage beast toying with his prey, Roland calmly drove to a filling station nearby the murder scene and parked right next to the pumps. Witnesses said he had a smile on his face—a pleasant smile for all he met—and he seemed super relaxed. And just as calmly as a man coming from church in a nice suit and tie, he then interacted with everyone he met inside the station's shop after filling the car with fuel.

Roland walked around serenely, got a cold soda, and began drinking it as he walked around the store looking at items. The woman who worked there said he hummed a little tune as he quenched his thirst, as thought it were just another ordinary day. He paused only once during his time inside the shop. The woman who worked there was nervous as she described how Roland "reacted" to a little girl who had just walked into the shop with her mother. Roland's mood soon changed from serene to furtive and on edge.

The shop keeper said she noticed Roland go behind the potato chip stand, kind of hunched over and looking through the items, as if to not be seen by the woman. At first, she thought he didn't want to be recognized by an ex girlfriend, and didn't think much of it.

However, as the little girl went past Roland with her mother, the shop keeper saw Roland reaching into his pocket. She said he went after the girl and put his hand on her shoulder and turned her around to face him, as he knelt down beside her. Roland smiled at the little girl lovingly, and asked her what her name was. He said she was a "special" little girl. The mother of the girl came over and stood nervously by her child, wanting to hear what was going on.

Roland then reached into his pocket and took out a gift for her child. He was so passive and soft spoken that the mother never questioned why a stranger would want to give her child anything. He opened his hand and gave the child a gold chain that had a locket on it. He told her to take it and keep it until she was "older."

When the mother of the little girl stepped over to take the necklace in her hands to see it, Roland got all nervous and agitated, so she backed away and Roland told the little girl that he had to go then. When she looked down and saw the gold chain in her hand, she smiled up at this man who seemed to want her to have that present.

Roland then told the child's mother, as they walked away awkwardly, that it was okay, and that he was wealthy. He said that he enjoyed passing out gifts to strangers. They hurried to the door after Roland began to lovingly stroke the little girls' face. The mother acted all skittish, witnesses said, but Roland walked merrily out of the shop, still humming a tune. (Of course, we all knew who that necklace belonged to—to one of the murdered women.)

Roland then drove a mere half mile away from the gas station and broke into another elderly lady's home. Just ten minutes after he had been in the station with the child, there he was stealing some more items from some lady's house located right near the filling station.

The items he took were very odd. They included a lady's dress, a set of hosiery, a blonde wig from a party costume, and a pair of lady's shoes. Just forty-five minutes after Roland had been in the gas station handing out trophies from one of the dead women he had just murdered, he drove back past the very same service station a second time. This time he even waived to the attendant outside, who noted that Roland was coming from the opposite direction he had come from before. The truth was Roland was coming from the burglary of the old lady's home, and returning to where he had killed the three women in the woods . . .

Evidence at trial showed that Roland went back to the crime scene a second time. It was there that he dressed up as an old woman in the stolen items from the burglary. What he did to those women in the woods only God knows.

Apparently he spent a prolonged time with all three of the dead elderly victims, and all while he was dressed as one. He "re-posed" their corpses. He even did more damage to one of the corpses that had fallen over after he had propped it up. Evidence showed Roland kicked the corpse over forty times – *after* the women were dead! The indentations made in the corpse were from a woman's shoe, pointed in the front, which exactly matched the pattern of abuse on the corpse.

Roland then masturbated over the dead women, leaving the scene of his butchery only after he had spent time playing with them. Then, of course, he went down that same lane it all took place on, driving back to the gas station a third time.

This time, however, he was not the suave man in a nice suit who had so calmly and sweetly handed out gold necklaces. This time he was in a panic, as the car's engine cut off, and appeared terrified that he wouldn't be able to drive it, as it actually coasted without power into the station lot. Gone was any pretext of calm; Roland was near tears and panicked when he thought the car was not operable and he was stuck there. A mechanic who worked at the station helped him re-start the car after several tries. The man recalled later that he might have seen a pair of "messed up" women's shoes in the back of the car trunk area, but he claimed that Roland closed it up before he could see more.

Sergeant Rage announced with glee that there would be no shoes like those on the unit and that Roland was not allowed any wigs either.

Why did I hate that monster Roland? Because he was the type of monster who was actually in complete denial about his acts. In jail, that predator actually went around pretending he was such a nice guy to those he wanted to suck up to, while constantly preying sexually on any young guys he could. He had a habit of breaking down young guys and luring them into sex with trickery, while trying all sorts of devious shit on many of the others who came to the prison at the same time.

What made me sick to my stomach was how he paid for pediatric magazines so that he could look at small children and masturbate to the images. He did that in the last prison in which we were together. He was smart enough to know that child pornography was illegal and never allowed in prison, so, he found a way to have seemingly innocent pediatrician publications sent into prison instead.

Roland knew that he could see children in these magazines naked or half naked, and that was enough for him to masturbate over in his cleverly sick way. It was seeing him with those magazines that made *me* have to be the one to beat his ass during our last prison stay together.

I will keep this brief, but it is about why Roland and I were always destined to do a sick "dance" together, the one that would have him trying to murder me over this incident.

One day, the guard handing out mail saw the child pediatric care mags for Roland in the pile of mail that he was handling on my old prison Block. He got angry that this sicko was receiving them, so he decided he needed to be brought down a peg. Unfortunately, this guard also hated me, because of my escape from that prison in 1985, so it was easy for him to pick my sorry ass out to do his bidding.

So, one Sunday in August of 1992, when there was no lieutenant on B-Block, the guards on shift put me and Roland together in an exercise cage located outside the rear of B-Block. It was nothing more than a set up for us to entertain the guards in a good old fight. Instead of me fighting Bruce Lee and his karate moves, I was dealing with a guy clinging to me desperately, one who scratched me and bit me, all while I did my best to crack his jaw with my fists.

All that "karate" that Roland claimed he knew was just bullshit. When it came to physical brawling, the jailhouse, made-up karate, which you were taught by some other inmate, was far more effective.

At six foot two, and two hundred and twenty-five pounds, I was far superior to him physically at thirty, my age when we fought.

I made his mush out of his mouth with my fists, while he left a set of scars on my face that are still there today, just below my right eye, from the deep gouges he made with his nails. That is why, as soon as I saw that Roland was being put in the cell that was located only three doors away from my own, I knew that the shit between us was not over with. With Sergeant Rage running the show, it was about to get real dicey for both Roland and me.

When the guards left the pod, Roland came and looked at me through the bars of his cell door. I snorted in disgust that we had to be so close to one another, being only fifteen feet apart. When he recognized me, he laughed a sick little mocking chuckle at me. We both knew what would eventually happen, and neither one of us was going to say anything to the "po-po" about it. We each nodded at the same time, like a signal to the other that it was "game on." Roland then went silent.

A short while later, another guy was brought in by the guards. I silently prayed that they weren't putting one of those "shit tossers" on our pod. I hated being around the guys who had lost their minds. They threw urine or shit out of their cells all the time. It was horrible to live around the insane while in prison.

What followed next made my heart sink. The guy was someone I actually cared for: Keith. I knew Keith from Huntingdon prison. He was there before me when I first got to Death Row back in 1983. Keith was white, stood about six foot one, and weighed about a hundred and seventy-five pounds. He had sandy blond hair that was thinning, and he also wore eyeglasses. He was in physical agony, because his hip had been shattered when he had been shoved down a flight of metal stairs by a guard some years back. He was handcuffed at the time the fell, and could not brace himself. So he ended up shattering his right hip during the fall. He screamed and passed out soon afterward. I was shoved back into my cell that day, because I was standing right behind the prison guard when he did what he did to Keith. He kicked him in the small of his back and sent him flying down the steps. The guard thought it was a riot, and laughed his ass off. He only stopped laughing when Keith screamed for way too long from his injury.

It was a pitiful sight to see Keith hobbling slowly, with the guards pulling him along. His glasses were steamed up, and his hair was matted with sweat from the effort to get over to his cell, which was next to mine to my left. I called out, "You okay, Keith?" He answered back, "Yeah, Nick". Crippled or not, he, too, got stripped and ass searched like me.

With Keith right in the cell next to me, I could hear his painful groans though the mesh vent that connected our cells. I knelt down and I could see his feet through the mesh, as well. When the guards left, I spoke to him through the vents and told him who it was that I saw in the other cell across from us. I also said that I had no idea who was in the cell that had an inmate in it already.

Keith said he had to go to the toilet, so I left him and went back to the door to see who else we had to live with there on the pod.

It sucked when he had his case read aloud by Sergeant Rage. I'd rather tell how it ought to be told and ignore how he made it out to be.

My friend Keith . . . shit, there's no other way to describe him . . . I loved the guy in some ways, so yeah he was my friend. He was kind and gentle and actually funny to talk to at times. He had a wicked laugh, and I don't know what else to say other than he was a nice guy—one who had killed his best friend.

Keith grew up in a rural part of Pennsylvania, and he started doing burglaries with his childhood friend. Now, the guy Keith shot was someone he had grown up with, who he'd had sleepovers with as a boy, and shared many days at their respective houses together as children.

But when Keith and his friend got caught doing a burglary, Keith's friend informed on him, so he'd serve less time, and Keith took it very personally. He lured his friend to a river one night and shot him point blank in the back of his head. Just as Keith was climbing the bank of the river, a police officer appeared. He knew Keith from the area and asked what he was doing. Keith said, "I was shooting some rats." That single line became the headline at his trial.

Being caught red-handed shooting your childhood friend in the head, all because he was going to be a witness against you, made for a short trip to Death Row for Keith. Sergeant Rage said Keith could be sure not to expect a birthday card from his friends if he shot them all in the head like that.

I saw that man Keith pay over and over for what he did to his friend at the hands of some of the sickest guards in Huntingdon. I saw him suffer his own anguish about what he did whenever we spoke.

Once the guard broke his hip, Keith suffered and *handled* more pain than anyone I'd ever seen. The way he accepted his punishment and never once acted proud of what he had done made me respect him. Some human beings actually show remorse for years, in ways we never get to see. I saw it all in that man.

While I was remembering all that about Keith, I swear that when I saw who was being brought along the corridor to our cell pod next, I half blurted out to him, "Oh God, not *that* idiot'!

It was "Rump" who came next, and Rump was a great jailhouse name for that guy. His actual name was Ronnie. And to my immediate displeasure, I saw that he was being put in the cell right next to me to my right. *Great, now this guy will be on the door talking, or always speaking to me directly through the connecting air vents all day,* I thought. The guards hadn't even finished taking the guy's cuffs off when he called out "Hey Buddy" to Roland, and then talked about how shitty the ride over in the prison bus was for us all, and how he was hungry already.

In other words, Rump was a life long *inmate* whose only complaints or thoughts were going to be prison related. Literally, he was mentally retarded.

Let's go down the "little path of really dark shit" as Sgt. Rage said about Rump. Rump (and yes he really liked it when others called him that name), had an IQ of 81. I knew that because he boasted that he "beat" being labeled retarded previously, *only* because of his *actual* score. He proudly told us all one day that you had to have an IQ of eighty or less to be considered *really* retarded.

Ronnie was white, stood about five foot ten, and was an easy two hundred pounds. He had "cave man-like" features, with a low, sloping forehead and close-set eyes, topped off with thick, greasy brown hair. His hair was always combed into a pompadour, in a style from the 60s. He was very coarse and obtuse in speaking terms. Ronnie was a pain in the ass to live next to, because he was just so fucking stupid.

Other than having told my tale, Sergeant Rage really had fun broadcasting Ronnie's.

Rump grew up in a rural part of Pennsylvania with eight siblings. His mother was an abusive alcoholic, and his father at times locked Ronnie in a dog kennel that was filled with dog feces. He had to endure days of physical and mental abuse as punishment for being mentally "slow." He was even made to eat garbage to survive until he began running away and living in the woods. At age twelve, he lived in the abandoned cars or trucks left in woods near his hometown, and became as feral a creature as any human could. He was soon in and out of jail constantly for petty crimes, up until the age of eighteen. The newspapers reported that the man had one of the sickest, documented childhoods ever recorded.

In 1974, Rump was convicted of the brutal rape of a woman whom he attacked after hiding in the men's room of a bar late one night, while waiting for it to close. The physical abuse to the victim was horrendous and Rump was given fifteen years for his first serious criminal conviction of that nature. He would serve every day of his sentence, because he was considered too violent to ever be granted early release.

So, in 1989, after he finished serving the full sentence for his rape conviction, he went right back to the same bar and, again, waited until it closed. This time, however, he tortured and then murdered the bar keeper in the same place where it all began—*and* he stayed to have drinks afterward!

At age fifty-six or so, when he stood before me in Pittsburgh Penitentiary, he had been in prison, or juvenile detention, for forty or more of those fifty-six years of his life.

Rump was severely "institutionalized," and he was someone who would kill you without hesitation for the slightest insult. I used a lot of charm to stay ahead of him and to keep him at bay, because he was that pit bull who hung from a tree branch and wagged his tail if you hit him with a stick, because his teeth would be sunk into any thing moving.

Sergeant Rage said that he was *never* going to let Ronnie buy drinks for him in a bar, yet Rump seemed not to be offended at all by the comment.

Next through the door came Bobby, another one you had to watch out for because he was a big nasty biker type. Bobby weighed in at over three hundred pounds. He was well over six foot two as well, so he was a lump of a human being. The guy was mean as hell to deal with. He had black hair and black eyes to match. He wore a beard that was quite long, and his hair was long and greasy too. Remarkably though, he had very white skin, like at some point you could see that he was a nice-looking teenaged boy. He was long past that now though.

Old Bobby had a nasty habit of manufacturing all sorts of clever weapons, in the past, to try and kill other prisoners, and Sergeant Rage said he liked Bobby for that. I saw that bastard do some clever and devious things, and I wanted no parts of him. We had a mutual "non-feelings" kind of relationship. He would go along with anything done to me by others, but he himself would not take me on directly, since we had no beef between us that he could use as motivation.

Bobby played by the rules mostly, so we had this weird relationship, whereby, if it came down to it, he would only act if I became a threat or if I somehow crossed him. The only problem was, Bobby had severe schizophrenia and frontal lobe damage resulting from calcification of his brain. It was made worse by years of him using methamphetamine. It did not take much for him to "think" someone was talking shit behind his back, and for Bobby to then try and kill that person for it.

His newspaper clippings were unpleasant to say the least. The real version that was read aloud to us paled in comparison to what the man told others, so I have to tell you what you would have heard versus what the truth was if you let Bobby tell it.

See, I was standing in the individual cage that I was exercising in back in Huntingdon when Bobby told his version of his "pedigree" to another pair of wanna-be bikers standing in the cages that were next to his. They were new to Death Row and he was putting up a big front for them. Bobby starting telling these guys how this one time, this "dude" had ripped him off. So, he and two of his "soldiers" from his gang went over to dole out some justice for the punk over his debt. I was working out in my own cage then, and I acted like it had nothing to do with me, as Bobby went on telling his version of what happened.

According to Bobby, on the day I heard him telling tales in the cages, this "dude" was a real bad ass, and he had a reputation for all sorts of violence. Bobby went into detail about how big and menacing the guy was, but he quickly added how he, Bobby, liked that kind of thing, because he was a self described "beast."

Then Bobby's story got juicier, as he told them how he burst in on the guy while some hooker was sucking his dick in bed, and how they trashed the place before Bobby got down to work torturing the guy. He said he had to; it was to get the combination to his safe that they had found in the place. (Bobby side stepped how they killed the girl in his telling, I later noted.) He went on to get all upbeat in the big finish to his story, which was all about the loads of cash and drugs that they got from this "dude" in the robbery.

Sgt. Rage told a different tale.

According to police, Bobby, at age twenty-five, was already ravaged by schizophrenia. He convinced two friends of his to do a burglary. None of them were on motorcycles, roaring over there as a gang, during the event. Actually, they *drove* over in Bobby's mother's car. He was living with her in the basement, while shooting methamphetamine all day. He had a broken-down motorcycle, half in parts, sitting in the front garden.

The group, led by Bobby that day, drove around getting high and started looking for ways to get money. When they found an apartment that they thought was empty, they broke in to steal items. They found a man and his nineteen-year-old girlfriend asleep inside the apartment. This kind of crime was rare back then. Upon finding the two people in the apartment, Bobby and his two pals sadistically went to work on them. First they took silver duct tape and completely covered both victims' faces — save for holes for their nose and eyes. Then, police said, they wrapped electrical cords around their necks and began torturing and choking them.

Eventually, after toying with the man for nearly forty minutes, Bobby stabbed him repeatedly, then strangled him for good measure at the kitchen table, all as his nineteen-year-old girlfriend watched in horror. He then dragged the girl downstairs to the basement, where he beat her so hard with a wrench that it was left embedded in her head. Then he stabbed her repeatedly and left her curled up on the basement floor. With the victims still there, he and his two pals partied in the apartment, before leaving the next morning.

Bobby was tried and convicted, and several inmates even testified at trial as to the many times he had openly told them about the crime in made-up form. He stood there, unflinching, as he was handed his death sentence, and never once showed any emotion. Why would he?

In *his* "reality," Bobby had taken on a rival biker gang, and he had all this other made-up "reality" that he clung to in his head.

Now, all you had to do to get yourself murdered by Bobby "The Beast" was to laugh at the wrong thing, or at the wrong time. Once he wanted you dead for some perceived paranoid thought that came to him, that was all he talked about, thought about, or worked toward getting done.

This guy was so huge and so menacing that many of the staff were intimidated by his aggression. I stayed well clear of Bobby on most days. I saw that he was always looking at people suspiciously, as if they were thinking of doing him wrong somehow. It's very eerie to be around a mentally ill person who can squash you with his giant frame. The shame of it is, nearly eighty percent of all Death Row men have some form of mental illness, or brain disease. The ones with a disorder can be dealt with. The ones like Bobby, who have non-treatable schizophrenia, are the ones who are capable of the most bizarre behavior at any moment.

Of all the acts of anyone I witnessed, one thing Bobby soon did on our pod would never leave me. It makes me sick at times to even recall it. The fact that a guard let him do it and laughed over it is what makes it all the more sickening.

After Bobby went into his cell, they brought us Dave. Dave was a white guy who stood about five foot ten, and had a big old gut on him from sitting around eating snacks all day. At an easy two hundred and fifty pounds of fat, Dave was near to fifty years old when he was in the unit right then. With silvering hair worn short in a close-cropped haircut that was reminiscent of a 1960s' hair style, Dave was also from rural Pennsylvania. He was an odd sort. He had actually just been put back on Death Row for the third time for the same murder, when he entered the place.

Sgt. Rage clearly did not like Dave, and he loved sharing the story about how Dave had first been convicted in 1986 of murdering a handicapped child while stealing the donations given to the child at a charity event. It was an event that Dave and his brother had attended that same day no less.

That same night, Dave broke into the home with his brother in tow, and they ransacked the house for the money meant for the disabled child. When they found out that the child had awakened during the crime, Dave butchered the little handicapped boy (who would have never been able to identify them anyway).

On appeal, there was a technical error, and Dave was sentenced to death by a second jury during his second trial. Upon further Appeal, the conviction was again reversed, owing to faulty instructions given to the jury.

So then, he was given a third jury trial.

Well, thirty-six jurors later, and after his brother had gone into court and told them the same story for the third time of how Dave killed the handicapped child for money to buy drugs and whores, well then, he became "Bad Luck Dave" and was put on Death Row. Sergeant Rage said that of all the men whom he had to put in a cell that day, Dave was by far the one he wanted executed first.

I had only spent brief times with Dave, because he had made so many trips back and forth to court that I barely knew him. I had no issues with him other than one. He thought himself able to judge me for a sex crime, even though he himself had butchered a handicapped child. But let us not quibble about the details, Dave . . .

Dave was not the brightest guy, and, for some reason, he was really good buddies with Bobby. It was like Dave was a minion of Bobby's, and together those two butchers had an ersatz homosexual relationship, whereby Dave benefited from every witty thing that came out of Bobby's mouth.

The guards put Dave right next to Bobby, in the cell second to the end, of course. No sooner was Dave out of his cuffs and in that cell then he and Bobby disappeared into the vents for a lovely catch-up chat. I bet they were all aflutter for the one hour that they were apart downstairs, since both were on a prison bus together, all day, on their way there. They had sat next to one another on the bus, too, and had quietly chatted the whole time, like some old married couple. I did not have to hear the two of them speaking to know what they were saying. As a partnered pair, they were already chattering about who the guards were putting in the cells around "them" and who "they" were going to have to be dealing with on the pod.

I swear, it was so weird to see a man act like he was married to some guy who he had never even known before prison.

At that point, I was just hoping that those who went into the last two cells weren't some of the men who were on the "hit list" of any of those guys I was already locked up with on the pod. It was a place where no one had a a chance of being left alone, because of the bad blood that arose from such close confinement. Unlike the old style prisons where everyone faced in one direction, this "pod" was like a fish bowl--one full of sharks looking to prey on the helpless. *There's no way this won't be a feeding frenzy,* I thought. Just then, *pop* went the door, and we heard them coming in with our latest new "chum."

The next man did not walk into the pod; he was rolled into the unit in his wheelchair. It was George. Oh man, if there was ever a case for the "worst life ever" argument, George was the guy who would have won it, hands down. Standing upright, he was about five foot six inches tall. He had bright orange hair and freckles. He was obese and had terrible acne scars — a white guy in his early thirties, who looked like he had dementia.

I had never before seen fingernails as long, nor as filthy, on another human. He was a wretched mess. Although I was not there at the time it happened, the story was that George went to court on appeal, walking like a normal person, but, after his trial, he came back to Death Row in a wheel chair.

Rumor had it that they sodomized him with a riot club and damaged his internal organs, along with breaking some bones in his back. The story George told didn't make any more sense than the others he told over time. All I knew was that he was crippled then, and he was one of the saddest cases I'd ever seen.

According to Sergeant Rage and his newspaper clipping collection, here was how poor George Boy got there:

The police said that in 1987, George was convicted of murdering his girlfriend, and was caught red-handed eating her flesh when he was apprehended. Yes, he was literally still lying on top of his victim, and cannibalizing her, when the police dragged him off her. He had been drinking and doing drugs with his girlfriend, when they had an argument. George began to violently assault her. Her screams were heard by many in the small community in Eastern Pennsylvania where they both lived. As the fight evolved into a serious attack behind a bar in an alley strewn with garbage, police were called to the scene.

When they got there, George was sitting astride his now-dead girlfriend, and was eating her breasts. By the time they pulled him off, he had eaten an entire breast and most of the second one. The police immediately became ill at the sight of what he had done to his victim. George don't tell his story to anyone. In fact, he drank prison "hooch," and took pills to blot out what he had done.

George was probably the most docile *sober* person I have ever met. Meeker than meek, he was obviously diminished mentally. That fact, combined with the many years of abuse he suffered, in and out of prison, had left him as ruined a human being as any I'd ever seen. He was so easy to manipulate that others often abused him sexually, or took whatever possessions and/or money he'd had sent to him from outside.

Why was he like this? Well, George was raised in a house where his mother was "ultra Christian." She was religiously driven to remove from George those evil spirits she thought made him slow-minded. When she found that he wet his bed at night, she would make him kneel on shards of broken glass and read the Bible for hours the following day.

His father often beat him with a metal rod taken from a fence, and even put tape on the handle to improve his grip. When he broke the rules, George was left in a box for days, and had to drink his own piss to survive.

Authorities said that the age of fourteen, George was so messed up mentally from that type of abuse that he ate a pet cat while it was still alive. It happened while he was sitting with this pet that he had been playing with in front of a neighbors home. He was so high on the glue he had been inhaling in front of the house for hours that he told people he did not remember any of it.

The only reason George did not receive any mental health treatment, and wasn't put away for life, nor even spared the death penalty, was due to the local prosecutor who handled his case. The prosecutor wanted the "cannibal case" to be bigger than just that of some mentally deranged human who'd been out of his head on booze. No, that would not have served anyone's career move!

So, they took the most pitiful person ever, and they put him on Death Row, in among men who loved having someone that weak to play with.

All I can say is that I felt sorry for George when I read what his parents had done to him as a child. But I had no time to pity him, because I had woes of my own. That man did the hardest time of all, though, and many enjoyed making his life hell. I just stayed out of it.

George got stuck next to Roland in the second cell, and they got along fine, mostly because George was easily manipulated, and Roland was able to get food from his food tray when they were served.

Two minutes after the guards left the food trays, I heard Roland already "working" George for whatever food items he was not allowed to eat, or did not care for. Roland offered George his fruits, and George gave him, like, ten items in return. Life could be so petty and cheap that something as simple as getting extra food from George was a real important thing for a con man like Roland. He knew he had struck gold with the "fool's bartering" that he had just done. Like I said, they all preyed on George.

Once they put that seventh guy in the last empty cell on our pod, the guards went on to fill up the next pod, located across from ours on the unit. Soon after they slid our pod doors shut on either side, it was Dave who pointed out that the guy who was already in the one cell between his and Rump's was Gary.

It all began when Dave called out to Rump, "Look who we got in our pod!"

I knew we had one leftover guy in there who had been at Pittsburgh all along. I went to my door to listen to Dave and Rump. All of us, except George, were standing at our doors when Dave started calling out to Gary, saying he should come to the door and talk to us about that place. What was the routine there? he asked. Gary ignored Dave, and we all sort of chuckled at Dave for being ignored.

I am only describing what Gary looked like for now. There was a reason they left him at Pittsburgh Penitentiary, and there is a reason that I am leaving out why he was sent to Death Row for a bit. You'll understand why later.

I had never met the infamous Gary before then, because I had been in a different jail than he was. He was someone whom I personally knew nothing about. Since Gary was there first, Sergeant Rage hadn't given us a big introduction to him anyway.

Once all forty-eight cells were filled with men who were like those I've described here, they soon served all of us food. There was a lot of hustle and bustle, as had our personal belongings given back to us, and were also issued the prison items for our cells. Then, after an hour or so, they explained the new routine to all of us.

These were the "rules::

1. Because of the limited space, four men would be put into a cage, outside, on the top of the roof, for exercise two hours at a time. No more would it be one man to a cage, (like it was back at Huntingdon). This would be four men at a time in a ridiculously small cage. There were four cages outside. *This is going to be madness!* I thought.

2. If you did not want to be outside in the cages (taking your chances with three sick-minded killers and no guard to watch over you in a cage), you could have two hours of

"day-room" time. That was the enclosed area in front of each of the three pods located on the south side of the unit, where I was housed. The other three pods had no metal tables or stools in them for day-room.

3. There was one phone in the day-room on three pods. If you wanted to make a call, you had to negotiate with the other three men who were put in the day-room with you for the two hours of time allowed. It was up to you to be able to get your own share of time on the phone.

4. You were allowed to come out of your cell and go into the shower area three times per week. You would not be handcuffed while out of your cell, but if you left the pod for exercise or any other reason, you were handcuffed in front.

5. You were allowed two hours per week in the "law library" with one other man. This was a set of secure rooms that had law books in them. It was also where men helped one another with their legal problems (and, so they said, was also where some prisoners sometimes performed sex acts on one another).

6. Nothing left the unit. That meant that whatever happened on the top floor of that place stayed there. If you broke that last rule for any reason (and made those men risk losing the easiest job they ever had), you would suffer like never before.

Now all six of those rules were shouted at us by the unit Sergeant, "Sergeant Rage," as he came to be known to us all. He always had to shout things loudly. He also always wore those big, thick-soled boots on his feet, so he could be at least at someone's chin level. He was a nasty mouthed bastard of a man with bright eyebrows and matching mustache that made him look like Captain Crunch, who was now a prison guard. He was about a hundred and forty pounds of constant trouble who stood about five foot seven.

Sgt. Rage loved the place. To be frank, it was his playground. Not a single inmate's letter went out that that wasn't read first by Sgt. Rage. And not a phone call was made that he and his boys were not listening in on.

If you got a juicy letter from a lady friend, Sgt. Rage got on the intercom in your cell and read it to you, while saying how hard her words made his dick get. If you wrote something about his unit to anyone on the outside, he read that to you as well, all while telling you how you were going to pay for your fuck-up.

One memory I have of him was of his reading my mother's letter to me one day soon after I got there. Stupidly, I pushed the button on my intercom and told him how he was making my dick hard, along with his. He and his favorite goon of a guard broke two of my lower teeth for that. I did not push the button many times after that incident.

The unit had a lieutenant who showed up from time to time, when he left his office, which was located out in the hallway. He was a wanna-be "pretty boy" with a weight problem. He had bars on his shoulders because he had a college degree.

The lieutenant was a white guy from the Pittsburgh area, which we knew right off, judging from his accent. He was about five foot nine, and weighed close to two hundred and fifty pounds. This was a guy whose ass was in a chair all day. He had normal shoulders and legs, but his ass was huge! He was also dating a nurse in the jail at the time, and he felt like he was a "Big Man on campus" for that reason.

I learned one true thing while doing time in the joint, and that was that the higher you were in rank, the more someone else did your job. That guy was so lazy that he had everyone doing his job for him.

Only thirty years of age, that guy, who was our unit lieutenant, was going to be a total blob of a human by the time he reached middle age. He actually ate trays of food, meant for prisoners on our unit, by having the kitchen send up fifty-two meals for only forty-eight men on his block.

Basically Sgt. Rage ran that place along with four men who were his best drinking buddies after work, while the lieutenant signed off on all of it. Sgt. Rage had it made then, as his minions would jump to work with him on any prisoner with their clubs or fists. The one thing that we were made to understood, over and over, was that no one told what happened on that floor beyond those men.

Now, I had just come from a prison that had been shut down after the United Nations had gotten involved by condemning it for its "active practices of torture." I was really disillusioned, because right away I could see that this place was clearly going to be worse than my previous situation!

I had just served twelve of the hardest years of my life in a prison unit called "B-block." Men housed in that place had an average rate of survival of just five years.

This was not making sense to me. I was sitting on my bed, wondering how this had all come about, when it became obvious. My heart sank when I saw they had put us all into the hands of prison guards who, themselves, were considered the "worst of the worst."

I will tell you now that I consider myself "lucky" that over the course of the next three years, I got out of there with *only* eleven broken bones, razor slashes on my neck and face, and *only* having two of my teeth broken. I was *lucky*, I tell you. That's damn right, folks. I am one of the lucky ones who was able to get past all of this, and lived to tell you how I handled such a nasty ordeal.

3

"Let the Lions Loose!"

O kay, so on my "little pod of murderers" that I lived on in 1995, we had Roland, George, then Keith to my left. There was my cell in the center, followed by Rump, a still-silent Gary, and then, finally, Dave, with Bobby, to finish off the guest list to my right. The daily set routine went something like this:

Each morning began with a 6:30 a.m. wake-up, head count. "On your feet and show some teeth!"

At 7:00 a.m. the sergeant would come past and open the "pie holes" on all eight cells. As he did that, he wrote down on a clipboard the names of those who wished to exercise outside in the cages versus those who wanted to take their chances in the day room. He also would collect outgoing mail from the doors.

Right behind him came those aluminum carts that were about six feet high, with steam coming off them like a locomotive train. They were full of food trays. The guards came into the pod pulling carts, with each guard holding a huge steel pitcher of coffee in his free hand.

First a guard would slide a tray into the cell through the pie-hole, then move two cells ahead. A second officer behind him had a huge pitcher of coffee in his free hand,

and would pour a cup of coffee. He would then place a tray into the cell that the first guard skipped, and that way they kept things moving fast. They went past *one* time, and you got what you got *one* time, because that train did *not* slow down. If you missed anything, or got a tray that an item missing, you shut the fuck up.

In came the tray, and out went your cup for the coffee, then, *slam!* they closed the "pie hole." No stopping, and your bitch ass fingers had better grab that cup quick, or it too got slammed shut in the "pie hole." They were *that* brutal—"Frick and Frack," those two officers, who were daily visitors to the unit. They were both huge and menacingly similar.

At 9:00 a.m., after they had collected your trays, it was "exercise time." You either took part in, or watched for the next two hours as four men exercised in the day room in front of your cell. According to law, twenty-two hours in the cell, with two hours out of the cell, five days a week, was "fair." All four men were meant to exercise in a ten foot by ten foot, square, caged area outside.

However, Pittsburgh had no room for that. Instead, men would enter an indoor area with a big metal table in the center, and metal stools around it. In other words, they all sat and played cards, or stood and talked to men locked in their cells on these "day-room pods" during that period. They would shout loudly over one another, in as rude and as uncaring of a manner as one could imagine.

It was in the day room where most of the murders would occur. The "outside exercise cages," filled with up to sixteen men divided between four cages, were actually safer than the day-room. In the day room, a man could slip a knife to your enemy, or any other small weapon that could fit through the heavy wire the cage was made of. Then you would be stabbed, while the guy who gave your enemy the blade laughed it up.

The day room was also where you could get boiling hot oil or other substances thrown in your eyes by an inmate who was out for his shower, while you were stuck in the day room cage.

You could also get stomped to death in the outdoor cages by the three other men in there with you, if they all turned on you at once, but there was less of a chance of that happening in there.

Oh, and you could also be raped in the cages by two men, while the third companion kept watch for a guard who might come to break it up. I witnessed that once, when a guy named William was raped by two guys in the cages with him, just days after we got first got there.

Now, if you didn't come out of your cell, you didn't get a phone call. If you wanted that phone call, you had to come out and "play" in the day room. I don't know how the others felt, but the idea of me talking to my mother, or someone I loved, on the phone, felt ugly right then. Especially while three predators circled around me, all waiting for their share of time on the phone—or for the opportunity to kill me.

You didn't dare slip up and turn your head around toward the mesh wire, or lean down at the base of the phone to try to hear clearly. What I mean is, you didn't try to speak quietly to the party on the phone with your back to anyone. If you made that simple, stupid move, and someone saw the back of your neck sticking out . . . you were done. You NEVER turned your back on anyone while inside the day room — ever! Not once.

Most days, by one in the afternoon, all the drama of inmate movement was over and they shut the whole place down by three. That was it. There was just a skeleton crew on after that, and no one moved on the floor. They turned off the day room lights by five, and you were locked down for the night.

Once we were locked down is when you'd notice the constant noise in the vents the most. When all forty-eight cells were filled up with prisoners, each one of the men did what I did, and blocked up the eighteen by twenty-eight-inch air vent that blew right down onto their bed. If you were the only guy who did *not* block your vent, you had a thirty-mile-per hour breeze blowing down on you all day. In summer, it was cold air, so you froze your ass off if your vent wasn't covered. During the winter, it blew hot, and you baked, had nose bleeds and headaches, and your skin turned "ashy" from being dried out constantly.

In order to block the vent in your cell, you made "squares," about three inches in diameter, out of toilet paper. You soaked them in the sink until they could be molded. Then, you would mash them against the metal mesh wire inside the vent opening, forcing the paper into whatever crevices there were in the metal until it stuck in there. It took a roll and a half of toilet paper to cover the thirty-six squares of the vent.

And still the noise from the giant air ducts roared all day long . . . The one time the noise actually came to a halt was really what kicked everything off on our pod. It led to the death of one of seven of my companions, just four months after I got there.

When you were denied TV or radio for breaking the rules, (or when some guard just wanted you to go sixty days without them just to torment you) you were at the mercy of the other seven men on your pod. They could could make sure you *had* to hear them all day long. And you could do *nothing* to block out the sound of their "mind fuck" efforts, unless, of course, you wanted to flush your toilet four hundred times in a row.

Gary was the first to endure the painful efforts by the seven fellow prisoners on our pod. It happened when he had nothing in his cell except sheets and a towel. It was then that we tortured him.

One day, during my first month there, Gary took "too long" going to the shower, stopping to get all chatty with another inmate named George. He was telling George about not talking to the black prisoners on the pod, indoctrinating him with his racist bullshit. Gary's doing that in our unit that day was enough to anger the guard on duty, so the guard put him on disciplinary time for "refusing to obey a direct order."

Oh how we all loved getting our digs into Gary then, and we sure delighted in making him feel low for the things he had done to end up on Death Row. He had to sit in an empty cell, listening to us talking about his crimes and laughing at him for hours.

We all knew his story, and nobody liked Gary. Fuck Gary, we all thought. He endured sixty days of us telling his story to each other, all while mocking his loony mind. Anyway, we taught Gary something when we did that to him.

Gary knew from being there before we got there, that when we all had no radio or TV, how he would get back at us. The way we had tormented him was nothing, compared to how he would get back at all of us, at once, for what we did to him.

Our prison was very old, and was located on the banks of the huge Ohio river. Well, rivers flooded, didn't they? And Gary knew that from being there before any of us. Actually, the city of Pittsburgh is built at the confluence of *three* rivers. So, basically, every winter, we experienced some power cuts due to the flooding that we had to deal with inside the jail. (I wasn't very keen to learn all of that in my first year there.)

It wasn't until the next time the power went out that I sincerely regretted fucking with my man, Gary. He taught me a lesson about delighting in the suffering of others with his own *schadenfreude.* I hoped he would rot in hell, twisting in agony for it, too, the nutty bastard . . .

The day it all happened, and how you will *now* get to learn about our buddy Gary and his back story, was like this:

Everything went dead. No lights, no noise, nothing. Then the security lights popped on and we were all bathed in their yellowish glow. I thought, *Oh shit, wonder how long we gotta go without power, and what the hell has caused it all to cut off?* That was when everything had gone silent initially, about 6:00 a.m. one morning. My ears were instantly ringing, like I had just came out of a rock concert. You could actually hear silence in that moment. I got up off of my bed and looked out of my cell door to the control unit, through the glass panels of the hallway.

Only the emergency lights were on, so in the dim yellow light, I saw the officer was walking "180" (as we called it). He was scanning back and forth to keep check on the three pods of the six that were on that side of the unit. He was able to see, but he could not activate the intercom to hear anything inside of the pods. I tugged on my door to see if it had popped open when the electricity shut off. Nope. Nothing.

Everything was so still and quiet that no one spoke for quite a while. All of us were so aware that we lived in an abnormal setting that we were stunned when the constant noise we were used to just ceased. We waited so long to see if the power would come back that it was like a quiet waiting game.

That was when Gary came to his door and began to torment all seven of us. Now, finally, I want to explain about his background, and why it was so important to wait until now to tell you about it. It makes me sick to my stomach, even now, to recall it.

What Gary did to other human beings was never motivated by the things that others go to prison for doing. It wasn't for sexual needs, nor "power over others," for the mere act of dominance. That was too common for the likes of this madman. He had a plan that was insane, one

56

given to him by God almighty no less . . . and here is how it all unfolded:

Gary went to prison in 1979. While inside, he made stock trades from his cell and good money in the silver and gold futures markets. He was receiving disability payments monthly from the U.S. military as well, after being diagnosed with schizophrenia, and he used that money while in prison to invest in stocks. By the time he left Graterford prison in 1983, he had accumulated nearly half a million dollars.

Now, the way I heard it (from guys I did time with who knew him then), he'd been done wrong many times by black prisoners while inside. You see, Gary was in jail for the worst crime he could have been incarcerated for, when it came to being locked up inside prisons that were dominated by black inmates. The reason Gary had a hard time in jail was because he made a *huge* mistake by victimizing someone on the *outside* who was black.

How did that happen?

In 1978, Gary went to a New Jersey mental institution and signed out his black girlfriend's mentally impaired sister from the hospital. He then put the poor woman in a cage in his basement, where he sexually abused her for hours at a time, just for fun, while holding her captive.

When she was finally rescued by authorities and returned to the hospital, they found she had not only been sexually abused, but was also pregnant with Gary's child.

Gary was given a sentence of three to seven years for the crimes of unlawful imprisonment and sexual assault.

He also paid a fellow inmate to help him get his time reduced on appeal, so that when the crack epidemic hit America in 1982 (and the prison population exploded from a million prisoners to two million seemingly overnight), Gary was released early in 1983 with all that money from his stock trades.

Once on the outside, he was determined to get revenge on every black dude who had raped him in jail. He was going to get even with anyone who had ever done him wrong as well. You see, the man truly was insane. No one had any idea what he intended to do once he was set free after that first jail sentence. He moved right into the heart of a black neighborhood in North Philadelphia, and set up a new place for torture and sexual amusement. He even bought a broken down Rolls Royce from the police impound yard auctions. He had a Cadillac engine installed in it to make it run again. Buying the car, just like everything else he did, was all for a reason, and part of his plan to start "hunting."

At the time, Gary was in his forties, and cleaned up enough that he could use his appearance (and the car) to start picking up black prostitutes. Tall, with dark hair, he was also over six feet tall. He groomed the women he wanted to keep, and made sure that they would not be sought heavily if they were to go missing. He learned all he could about the women he wanted by researching their backgrounds. He even purchased a mail-order bride from the Philippines, whom he married, and immediately began pimping on the streets of Philadelphia.

After cocaine use had made his already crazy mind worse, Gary went berserk and beat his new wife nearly to death. She and her unborn son soon fled the house and police nearly found his "Den of hell" under the house right then.

That was when he lost it.

Gary went to the "next level." He finally came out of his shell and showed us who he really was. He started collecting "slaves," one by one, until he had five of them held hostage in the basement of his house. He dug a huge pit in the basement, deep enough so they couldn't climb out.

The women Gary abducted all had to be able to produce children for him. That was very important, since he had lost his new, half-cast child when his mail-order bride fled. When he found out that none of the women he had abducted could bear him a child, he went berserk.

Gary electrocuted one victim to death, and strangled another, right in front of the others, because they had lied about their ability to give him children.

The three remaining women were then put on a diet of dog food, which he mixed with the human remains of the victims he had killed, preparing it himself in his kitchen. He abused them for months, trying to breed them in the filthy pit they were made to live in. I couldn't imagine how those poor women endured what he did to them.

And to think I lived three cells away from that guy, and could see him every time I stood at my door, when he was at his door at the same time, while we were getting our food trays.

I walked past him daily, and shared the same re-filtered air as he did when we stood next to one another during those times our cells were searched weekly. We would look at one another, but never speak. He knew better than to try his racist shit on me, based on the looks I gave him. I was glad that I had been in on that first incident, when we messed with him early on, when he had no TV or radio. Doing that spared me having to interact with him on any kind of personal level afterward.

I did not have long to enjoy the elation I'd felt that day when we lost power though. And, to my horror, (you can look it up, because it was big news that particular year) all three rivers overflowed their banks that winter, and the entire sub-basement of Pittsburgh Penitentiary was submerged in water. The power generator of our building was underground, which meant that it, too, was submerged. It took days for the flood waters to recede, so power in the building was cut off and we went without energy for a total of nine days.

Gary did not have a just a few hours to get back at us; that shit was about to go on day and night for*ever,* man. It was so bad that, at some points, men grew hoarse from screaming at him for what he was saying.

Here is another example of how Gary's little performance set us off:

He put on the "performance" of a lifetime alright, taking center stage, and ripping on us for over a week. He would start off in that mocking tone he used to mimic the terrified voices of his "victims," who had lain in chains while inside his basement torture chamber. He painted a picture of them conversing about him, and how he knew what they were saying all along, as he lay for hours on the floor above, listening through a hole that he had cut for just that reason.

The first voice he used was deep and powerful. I can still recall every detail, even when I try my best not to. I'll never never forget how he did it:

"God gave me my slaves!" he'd say. Then, switching to a falsetto impersonation of the first victim soon after, he'd continue, "Oh, girl, this man crazy. He gonna kill us all. How we gonna get out of here . . ."

Then, Gary, in the slightly deeper falsetto voice of a second woman, answering the first, "Shhh, please don't let him hear us talking, honey. I am just praying to God he is gonna stop!"

And that was when Gary would use his own, natural "overview voice" again, taking the image he had just painted in those victims' voices, and driving it deeper as the narrator of his sick tale.

With mocking laughter, he told us how he was going to kill them, hoping that we would be forced to imagine how he had tortured those black women. Then, he drove home his point further, telling us how he laughingly played out his sick ritual on them because they were his "black piggies."

He always began with a snide laugh that was purely "put on," before saying over and over: "I own you bitches by *right,"* and then, "I am going to teach you why God chose me above all men to breed you!"

(By that time, he knew enough to wait until whatever screamed obscenities had died down before continuing.) "I am your MASTER, you filthy niggers! God put me here to use you to create the MASTER race!"

He went on to explain how the "mud" people needed to be bred off the earth, in favor of a superior seed. He told the victims that their only hope was to be made pure by having him and other white men breed a master race.

At first, I would kick the cell door along with the others. I flushed my toilet like they did, too, and drove my fingers into my ears to try and blot out his voice, no doubt as the others did as well. None of it worked.

Why not? Because, if you can imagine it, the guards actually helped Gary by pulling out the ones who were kicking hard on their cell doors, and giving them a beat-down while he laughed about it!

Oh, sure, they let Gary keep right on with his crap, saying shit over and over without them saying a word. Why? Because they saw what he was doing, and they loved it. In one day, Gary was able to torment us ten times more than they could in a year.

So, if you kicked too hard on *your* cell door, *you* got YOUR ass whipped, before being tossed back into your cell—much to the delight of a laughing Gary. Or, you could do what I did, and just grit your teeth and take it as best you could.

Gary had it down pat. He had a set way to tell us what he did, but more importantly to him, we were exclusively privileged to know his plan in detail. Each time he performed his "routine," he had about fifteen good minutes to add in the most important bits.

By the third day of his unending performance, many had just given up trying to drown Gary out. But that didn't make him any less determined to drive it into our brains over and over.

When the nurse and the lieutenant came by, Gary would stop long enough to take his medications, and then he would be right back at it. I know it wasn't funny to think this shit back then, but, man, crazy people could physically go on for hours on end, whereas a normal person would wear down!

I mean, I can kick off in anger, but twenty minutes later, I am, like, "done with all that shit," and I'll just say "whatever" then and go on about my business. But crazy people like Gary have some sort of "monster, energy drink" thing going on in their blood. They can go for days repeating the same insane acts, or words, all while drunk on the power of some kind of shit that we know *nothing* about!

At one point, I questioned whether Gary might not have been worried they would finally put the lights and power back on, because he sure seemed to rush to get his act down without missing a word. He seemed to think that our favorite part of his overall performance was his describing how he had "juiced the bitch."

That was his way of describing how he wrapped an electrical cord around a woman's throat, plugging it into a wall socket to kill her. He delighted in telling how he had killed her (may God help me for sharing this) in the puddle of urine at the bottom of the pit where the other poor women were chained.

Gary made any black dude on that unit want to kill him for describing how that poor lady gurgled and flopped around on the floor like a big fat fish. I wish I could have gotten to him right then for how angry it made me just hearing him laugh about it. I felt really bad for those fellow prisoners born of black mothers, who had to hear that crap, before me, over those years.

I know it was bad, because I nearly cried in frustration by the end of it all. That was the sickest time of my life. Of all the prison stories I've shared, I've never gone into much detail about that one event. It makes me so sick to even recall it, that, for years, I resisted talking about it, I guess.

At one point during that week, I took time out to watch Gary perform his act, trying my best to not let it affect me. Gary struggled to make absolutely sure he had the details correct, so much so, that it appeared he was relating a fervent belief system that he had complete control of inside his mind.

I watched intently as he described grinding up a human being into food. I saw the sinister way in which he made a joke of chopping her up. I have to admit, I felt so much pity for the women that I could only imagine what it was like to be held captive by that guy, as I stood there before him.

I stood there transfixed, observing him in a detached way. I could just look at him, and picture him back in his basement, frothing mad with anger. I could actually see him unleashing all of his fury on his victims. It was as though, in Gary's mind, somehow, God himself had given Gary a mandate to create a new race by doing all of that sick shit—and it gave me the creeps!

At one point, I noticed that Gary really reacted to anyone mentioning his child, or saying how they were going to "get" his child in revenge, if they ever got out of jail. That was a sore spot with him, and he would really rev up his rhetoric, and react with venom whenever it was mentioned.

On most days, Gary had a favorite target—Roland—the only black inmate we had on the pod. In response, Roland kept asking Gary how his child was doing. At first, I wasn't sure which child Roland was referring to. But then Roland would shout about the handicapped woman Gary had raped, and that really set Gary off. Roland said he could not even have a male child, that he could only father female baby whores for other men to breed. Then, of course, Roland would ask where were the superior generation of supremacist kids that Gary had made. Why did they let their Messiah suffer?

I think Gary hated both his inability to father any male children with his captives the last time, as well as the fact that the two children he *had* sired (with his Philippine wife and his ex-girlfriend's abducted sister) were taken from him before he could poison their minds. When you see how that all came back to haunt Gary later on, it wouldn't have mattered what he said to Roland as a comeback.

When power was finally restored to the unit, Sgt. Rage knew we were all going to get back at Gary for his shit, so they moved him to the other side of the unit, well away from us all.

Everything was different for us, somehow, even though they moved him away. We all felt emotionally violated after listening, day after day, to a man describe with glee all the horrors you never want stuck in your head.

No one had anything to say for days, after Gary had finished bombarding our minds with his sickness. I guess that was his parting present to all of us for thinking that we had the upper hand over him.

That was the quiet time, right before we started making all sorts of sick attacks on each other in the unit. It was as though, because we could not take it out on the bastard who wound us all up, we then turned on each other instead.

Just as soon as we resumed our routines again, all manner of mayhem erupted. It was like Gary had ripped the lid off of a hornets' nest. Soon we were acting like the sickest bastards ever, because we had been used and toyed with Gary's shit by the staff.

Poor George was the first one to find out that the rules, as we knew them, no longer applied. He went into the day room soon after the power outage incident was over to try to use the phone to tell his family that he was okay. With very little provocation, Bobby got angry with him, and told him he wasn't touching the phone before Bobby had a chance to use it. George tested him by trying to use the phone anyway, since he had already gotten through to his family . . .

Bobby calmly let George get all the way through to his party on the phone, then stealthily walked over to where he was behind George in his wheel chair.

First Bobby took off his prison jumpsuit, along with his giant T-shirt, and stripped down to boxer shorts only. His huge hairy chest and belly were a shock to see against his super white skin. Then, he tossed his sweat-stained, T-shirt over George's head, and punched him about six or seven times in the back of his head to knock him out. It made me sick to see a man in a wheelchair being abused like that. Bobby began to forcibly sodomize George orally in the day room, right there in front of our cells. Roland was also in the day room, and thought it was so funny to watch, that, when Bobby finished, Roland took a turn abusing George, too.

Then, after Roland had a turn on George's face, Bobby wheeled the poor man over to where the phone was still dangling, and beat him in the head with the handset while shouting "Hell-O!!"to anybody still on the line at that moment.

When Keith saw a fellow, crippled inmate being abused right in front of his own cell, he had no doubt that he might very well be next. I was sure that he saw how the guards, who were in the control booth right at the moment of the attack, were also mimicking how Bobby had just face-fucked George. The guards were mocking them all in a parody, making believe they were doing to each other in the control booth, what the inmates were doing to one another in their cells. When Keith said to me in a pitiful voice, "This is too sick to be real," I knew that he felt that there was no hope for him now at all.

I wanted to pay back Bobby for what he had done to George, and I had already decided to do Roland wrong, the first chance I got, as a matter of self preservation. But first, somebody had to stop Bobby before he went way too far. If he wasn't stopped, it would only be a matter of time before he went through all of the others, and eventually found time to "play" with me.

I'll have to tell you about Gary's fate a bit later on, when you'll see how he ended up in a little insane procession to be the second of two men killed in Pennsylvania. But, for now, because of what happened to George as soon as power was restored, I'll finish with Keith's story now, and explain how he was the first guy to die—all because of that sexual assault on George.

I wouldn't have minded one bit if it had been Gary who went to his death first, but that was just me wanting to get him out of my head. Instead, after we were there for just a few months, it was Keith who was the first guy to die. And although his was the first death among the men I was housed with while inside of Pittsburgh Penitentiary, it is also the one I still struggle with most some nights . . .

4

Keith Took *His* Way Out

Keith was not built for that shit. The guy was *not* a monster, nor was he a madman, either. He was just one, single, stupid act in his life away from being you or me, folks.

In prison, there were four ways in which an average person like Keith could escape.

He *could* go on living with a complex belief system that would have him believe that eventually he *will* get out. One interesting phenomenon is that when you ask a guy on Death Row what his chances are of survival, he has a set way of telling you that if "this, or that happens" (or if the appeals courts only focus on what they say are the *real* points), he will be going home. He will not just be getting a lesser sentence, mind you, but he will tell you he will be going home—*period.*

Then, there are the people who come up with "The Blur," as I call it. For them, using things like watching endless hours of TV, or playing chess with another guy are common. Men will resort to all manner of things to stop themselves from thinking about how their lives are being crushed daily.

I knew of men who watched TV for up to eighteen hours a day, and, if they had no TV, quickly went dark mentally. It was as if that TV box was the only reality that they could deal with.

If none of that worked, you took handfuls of pills given to you by the staff for free. The little blue ones made you sleep for up to twelve hours a day, leaving your brain in a kind of fog. I saw men check out on the "Little Blue Express" as we called it, for years and years. Once you went down the pill route, you never came back to anything close to normal.

Last came religiosity.

Oh, the way men would all of a sudden fervently seek God, as a way to escape their fate with a new religious conviction. It didn't matter how many people they had butchered on the way to being convicted. All they needed to do was say some magical words and imagine themselves "being" in the sky, and they'd have their blood-stained deeds wiped away!

Those men would pop on a new head garment to pray with, after giving their parents' birth name the "heave-ho," and then get to sit next to their victims in the afterlife, all as a reward for assuming a new identity. Just like that, with some magic words spoken there on Earth, and WHAM! then they were forgiven.

Those men actually believed that they and their murdered victims were equal again in the eyes of God, just for adopting prayer. They'd all get to sit in harmony on a big bench somewhere in Heaven, forever and ever, amen.

I have seen some world class actors playing the "religiosity game" while in a cell. I have witnessed men trying valiantly to become pious by accepting God, in an effort to pay for what they had done. (I believe God is proven in the equation E=MC^2.)

No matter what, religion is still the last of the mentally driven escapes from prison that there is. I *never* believed my spirituality made me any better than any other person. All I ever prayed for was to be "good."

I honestly believe that having no way to "blur" reality (which truly could have helped him escape from that place) made Keith want to die right away. Gary's torturing us all for so long, combined with Bobby's showing how the guards were in on that sick joke of an experiment was too much for Keith. I think he was just incapable of coping with that zoo. He had no way to defend himself against the three other "psychos" in the cages or in the day room; he was helpless to stop anything.

Keith never had a chance. He lived in a place where just going to the shower, with his shattered hip, was agony, and also a good place for him to be hurt seriously by another inmate. He turned to me for answers for weeks, when we talked through the vents to one another, after the assault on George.

At the time, I was dealing with some pretty bleak shit of my own, because it seemed that one guards on the block had it in for me. I didn't know what started it, but the guy was making my life a living hell. So when Keith said he couldn't take it anymore, I offered to have some weed sent over from "population," or to get some tranquilizer pills from George, (or one of the others who took them).

I told Keith that he ought to just take some of his own pain pills, together with a bunch of other pills we could barter for, and just go quietly in his sleep. I even offered to make some jailhouse "hooch" for him, made from grapefruit sections and bread, mixed with sugar, and all sealed in plastic bags. That way, he could have a drink of booze if he wished. I told him we could have a nice party for him, and he could just check out of the "hotel" in a nice, sleepy way.

Keith said that, as a Christian, he was not able to kill himself, no matter how bad the ordeal was. He had to obey God's law. I told him that I would have to think about that.   I said I couldn't just strangle him, and I couldn't knife his ass, even if he wanted me to.   He laughed, of course, because he knew I was just cracking silly jokes.

But then, he said—as I had heard him say many times—"Oh, man, *why* did I do it?!" I knew then it was best to leave Keith be, because that was what he always said to himself, in retrospect, when he thought about why he had been so stupid as to kill his only childhood friend.

One night in the spring of 1995, after one of the many conversations that we had together (which was almost always done through the vents, as we lay in our beds at night), I crawled back over to the vent by Keith. I got close enough to where I could see him lying on his mattress, before I spoke.

We had pretty much stopped talking for the night, but because he was so down mentally, I was drawn to his side of my cell. I said, "I think you should hear something I've planned."

I could clearly see Keith's chest and lower body through the vent. He was lying half propped-up on his pillow on his bunk. Because of the shattered hip, I knew that he was in a lot of pain, and he had to lie on his side constantly. He was getting bed sores from lying on the side of his body without the fractured bones, which was the only side he could lie on.

I told Keith that I had also read the Bible several times through by then. I said that maybe I could help him in his search for answers, and about what I had planned. We talked for hours that night. I took breaks to make coffee at times, and I sat there going over and over it with him. I even got out the Bible and read a part to him that I knew *had* to make sense to him about the point I was making.

I did all that I could to really work on him. And, at the same time, I tried to make him strong in the ways in which he said he needed to be, in order to accept what I had to offer.

It was nearly morning when, in a croaking and very tired voice, Keith said that he going to try to get on his feet for head count. I left him to his wobbling efforts, and went and sat on my bed. I was so worn out from talking to him, that I stood up and began walking mindlessly back and forth, which I continued doing for hours.

Even though I was exhausted, I maintained my routine: five paces one way, a turn on my heel, and then four paces back. (Anyone who said they did five one way, and five back the other way was a liar. That's just how it was.)

All morning long, I kept walking. I knew that each hour of five-by-four steps equaled about a half mile. I wanted to sleep all that day, so I kept at it until after I was finished with day room. Once they started shutting the unit down in the evening, I slowed down, eventually stopping when they turned off the lights. I stripped out of my sweat-soaked clothes, then bathed in the sink and went to bed. I heard not one peep from Keith that whole day, nor hardly any more over the next few weeks, after that night.

One morning, it was the lieutenant who came on the pod to open all the pie holes, instead of Sgt. Rage. That was rare, and, of course, he had to be an asshole about what followed.

When he got to Keith's door he shouted, "Good morning you DEAD Motherfucker!" He followed that with "Oh *FINALLY!*" And then, lastly, he said, "I love this asshole. He's the *one!*"

I knew, before he had finished, what he was yelling about. I knew, even before Dave asked the lieutenant what was going on, exactly what was going to come out of his fat-assed mouth in reply to Dave's question. I did not have to wonder; I just *knew* what was coming.

The Lieutenant announced to all eight of us at once that his morning had been made ever so much brighter by the morning news broadcast. He told us that he'd just heard on the news that Keith had his death warrant signed by the governor. And what he liked best was that Keith was going to be put to death later that same month—May of 1995!

I was sick to my stomach that it was *that* fast.

I mean, we had just gotten to the unit a few months earlier when they changed the method of execution from electrocution to lethal injection. All the court battles weren't even over yet as to whether or not the state was allowed to even use this new method to execute prisoners. Now, all of a sudden, thanks, in part, to Keith, there they were getting the green light to carry out all of the executions by that new method.

Everybody kept quiet, because no one liked a member of staff to get all pumped up at one of our deaths. We may have all fought like a bucket of crabs among one another, but when the staff singled out one of us like that, we all knew we could be that "one guy," so we weren't about to let them make us join them.

I knew in my heart that Keith was as embarrassed as hell to not only have us learn the news, but also at how it came to them that morning. Soon, everyone would learn that all the shit was about Keith volunteering to go to his death, and how that was affecting their appeals.

Keith had decided to be the first man executed in Pennsylvania in twenty-five years, rather than live like that on my pod. That is what drove him. Keith also knew that every man on that unit would feel that he had just made it possible for all of them to be lined up and put to death next. He broke the stalemate that had existed for years, with the state unable to execute a prisoner. He broke the code and gave up first. He was the coward who had let every murderer feel closer to his own end in that way. They all felt that about Keith. It appeared to everyone that he had zero friends right then.

I sat on my bunk and did not try to speak to Keith through the vent after that incident. He did not answer any of the men who shouted at him for being a pussy, as they paraded past his door. Nor did Keith respond to the ones who begged him to "stop giving the man what he wants." When a prisoner like Keith had nothing to say to anything that anyone said to him, I learned that it meant that the man had his mind already made up.

So, when it all came, it came, oh, so fast.

In the blink of an eye then, the day came, with guards pouring into the pod real early in the morning to take Keith out of Pittsburgh, and to transfer him to his final destination at Rockview prison.

Rockview was in the center of the state, and was isolated as hell. That was where the old electric chair was located, and where they had a nice new method of sticking poison in your veins. Regardless of which method they used, the result was to end your life in that "Death Chamber" located within the prison.

It seemed as though it had only been a day or two earlier, when Keith had talked to me through the vents in our cells. Early on, when all the guys had tried talking to Keith about his decision to die, we thought it would drag out for months. There were dudes who came around the first day following Keith's decision who were ready to act. One even begged him to come to the yard so they could "snuff" him, if he "just needed to die."

I swear to God, the way they offered to murder him was as if they were doing him a favor by "hooking him up." Doing him this big *favor*?! Man, that was cold.

Then there was this guy named Frank, who was *really* afraid to be executed.

Frank was this white guy, who was about five foot nine, and weighed no more than a hundred and fifty pounds. He was convicted of repeatedly slashing a gay man's throat with a box cutter, some years back, in an area just outside of Philadelphia. One day, he was standing in the day room, outside of Keith's cell, when he spoke to Keith (who was lying in his cell with his cell light out, because he didn't want anyone to talk to him).

He said, "Keith, I know you can hear me . . . listen . . . I know you don't know me, but I have to tell you something." (Frank didn't wait for a reply, because he had rehearsed what he was going to say, so he plowed right ahead.) "Yeah, so listen, Keith, come to the law library tomorrow. I can slit your throat with a razor blade. I can even put your head over the waste bucket in the library so that the blood will be all inside of it."

There was a brief pause, and, again, there was nothing from Keith. Then, in an effort to have his offer to do the deed accepted Frank added, "You don't have to look at it or *nothing*. It will be over quick!"

But since Keith never replied to any of his shit, Frank seemed let down that his efforts to save us all from the hangman had fallen short.

Others were somewhat more blunt in their offers to "help" Keith.

There was a guy named "Busthead," who said he was going to kill Keith for wanting to die. The guy had been put on Death Row for killing inmates in the past, and I didn't even know his real name. He loved his jailhouse name of "Busthead" though, because he loved to do just that—bust people's heads.

At about five foot ten and weighing two hundred and thirty pounds, he was a round, brown bi-product of a "crack head" mother and a heroin-addicted father. Basically, Busthead was a giant ball of anger, the result of a nasty childhood spent in foster care.

One day, Busthead shouted at Keith from the day room, using a different tactic. He said that if he failed to get to Keith and murder him before the "police got him out of there," he was going to butcher Keith's mom, if he ever got out of jail one day.

When that failed to get a response from Keith, Busthead said he would have one of his boys, who were already on the outside, go over to Keith's parents' house next week. He told Keith he'd have his boys kill them all right then.

After loudly bursting into the day-room shouting for "this white motherfucker" to wake up, and ignoring anyone else in the area , here is how this maniac, Mr. Busthead so eloquently put it to Keith in a fast, machine-gun-type statement, all while standing in front of his cell, and doing jumping jacks for exercise:

"Hey, white motherfucking, cracker-ass devil. Get your motherfucking, honky ass up on your door, *now!*"

(That was half a notch higher than Busthead being his usual calm self when he was wanting to see someone at their door.)

That day, he was really at full throttle, screaming with anger driving him onward. When he found out that the white devil named Keith was putting him closer to his own "real death" (as Busthead described it), there was no fuckin' way *he* was letting that white cracker boy put him closer to *his* doom!

So there was Busthead, standing in the day room, demanding that Keith get his ass up so that he could explain to him how, if he went through with his white devil plan to "bring us *all* closer to dying," Keith better expect his mom and dad to die as well.

Keith never answered, and I kept my mouth shut, along with all of the others on our pod, the whole time. Busthead had already killed other inmates for less than that, so a week without a homicide stabbing was considered a slow week for him.

You knew that he was one crazy bastard, just seeing him before you, with his offset eyes, manic motions, set phrases of violence, all making him look agitated. He had this look, made complete by a shaved head and the "no regard for human life" smirk that he proudly wore on his face.

Trust me, the guy was something else. Oh, and by the way, he was "forcefully gay" without caring whether you were as well. (I'm just throwing that out there.) His favorite thing to do in prison was to grab a smaller man from behind, and punch him in the back of the head until he was out cold. Then Busthead would bend him over while pulling his clothes off, and orally eat his ass in front of others, and rape him.

Anyway, Keith knew that he was going to go through with his own sentence. He was going to be executed. So no threats by anyone there was going to make him fearful.

If it was me that was in Keith's shoes, I would have indulged myself by talking back. Oh, hell yes! If you knew you were "out of there," like my boy, Keith, knew he was, then take some shots, I would say!

I would have told Busthead to try and brush his big nasty teeth after he had just finished forcibly eating another man's ass. I would have definitely told Frank to go and slit his own fuckin' throat, and told him what a sick fuck that he was for even asking to do that for me. But hey, that's just me, I guess . . .

It went on like that for a while, with Busthead coming around for a few days taunting Keith. It never got beyond words though. No one was able to stop Keith from being put to death, no matter what ploy or threats they used. I was on a mission mentally to stay well clear of it all with the other men when they tried to get me to talk him out of it. In fact, I did everything I could to blot it all out. I stopped talking to Keith for days and left him to himself. I felt like there was nothing else I could do at that point, anyway.

On the morning they came and moved Keith out of the cell on the pod, not one person spoke during the whole thing. Even the dickhead of a lieutenant from our pod was quiet, because they had all of these officials on the unit making sure everything was all captured on camera.

A procession of six officers and two sergeants, as well as two lieutenants, came this time. The deputy Warden was there as well.

They came in a long procession, with one of the officers holding a shoulder-mounted camcorder behind them. All of the men were very quiet on the unit, as the deputy warden told Keith that it was "time." He spoke the only words that were spoken: "Keith?" Then, "It's *time.*" That was it.

He waived his arm in the air to signal to the control booth, Keith's door popped open, and they went in to get him. There wasn't a sound, as they emerged with him in chains. At that moment, my balls shriveled up in my nut sack, and I stood at my door with my fingers gripping the mesh in the slots, and my forehead resting on the cool metal door. I wanted to to stand like that until Keith came by, but I kept going over and sitting on my bunk momentarily, only to pop right back up and stand at the door again. It was really nerve wracking for me to see him that one last time.

The guards had obviously gone into Keith's cell and, with a bit of care, helped him up, it seemed, from off the bed where he always lay. They came out of the cell with him, an officer on either side, each holding an arm, Keith wearing handcuffs, his hands meekly in front of his body.

Keith's eyeglasses were askew on his face from the effort to get up, so he kind of ducked his head to the left to even them up as he passed my cell. I got a knot in my stomach, as I watched him take the last footsteps of his life. I made eye contact with him there and then. Just as I was about to say *whatever* it was that never came out of my mouth, Keith beat me to the punch.

Of all the things I would have expected him to say to me, what he said was totally unexpected. He simply and sweetly said, "Thanks, Nick." That was all that I got from him.

I nearly shit my pants, and all the blood drained from my face, as I went over and sat the fuck down. I fled as fast as my wobbly legs could carry me from his words. That shit blasted in my ears and made me run. I didn't even say goodbye or anything, when he hit me with that line.

Looking into a man's face as he walks to his death freaks you out. It's as though they touch some secret "thing" that you never want to acknowledge. They are going to a place where you are fighting to never go, and it creeps you out to your core to know you have to go as well. Their willingness to go to that place makes you feel ashamed, and scared for feeling that you know it is coming your way soon. Yet, you never want to admit it.

I felt this awful chill pass by me when Keith and the execution team went by my cell door. I don't think the chill I felt had anything to do with the temperature, either. I swear that it felt like a huge ball of death, or whatever "death" is, had just rolled menacingly past me. I was afraid of it, whether it was real or not.

At the door of the pod, as they all left with Keith, I heard the officer say "MT" to the control booth officer. Those were the two letters they put on top of your cell door to replace your name, which was written on the cell door in blue-colored name cards. All of our names were laid out on a board taped to the control panel, located inside the booth. Keith's was now gone, replaced by "MT" on that spot.

We got no exercise for a couple of days following Keith being taken out to be executed. They wanted to give us all time to process his death, and even had the unit psychologist come around to speak to whoever needed it. I gave that a pass.

The lieutenant thought it was "cool" to have the front page of the newspaper, with the story of Keith's execution on its cover, mounted and framed. He placed it in his office, so each time we were taken out of the pod to the main hallway, we all saw it hanging there.

I should have known that the newspaper on the wall inside the lieutenant's office was a bad omen.

By doing that shitty thing, the lieutenant magnified everything negative, and the guards began acting like the shit was "real," with executions being carried out. It made all the guards feel that since everything was so real, they could just *"get it on"* with doing more crazy acts on "those motherfuckers!"

They held us all in our cells for a few days after the incident, hoping to calm us all down. Yet that next week when they resumed our "routines" on that unit, after Keith was executed, all hell broke loose. In one week alone, we had five straight days of serious violence occurring.

That was also the week I made the most bitter enemy of a guard there. I did not do a single thing to provoke it either. I did not need to, as I had that cocksucker, Roland, on the pod scheming to get me. He now wanted to carry out *his* plans to finally see if he could murder me.

5

The Worst Place to Shut Your Eyes

How the hell I managed to get through this next bit still makes me proud of myself, on one hand, while, at the same time, making me want to shake my head in shame.

It was halfway through the first, day-room period on a Monday morning after Keith was executed that I heard the sounds of a fight kicking off in the pod next to ours — the sounds of running footsteps and keys jangling, combined with the very distinct sound of metal clubs on flesh, with those *thumps*, low down in the sound range — sounds we were familiar with in jail.

I looked out my door and saw two, bloody, messed-up guys being pulled apart. I couldn't tell who was fighting with whom, but soon word spread from vent to vent, and the guys on my pod were saying it was guys fighting over the phone.

No big deal.

Then Busthead knocked a guy named Donald out cold with one punch, inside of one of the cages outside, and was stomping hard him, until the guards rushed to save him.

The next day, the unit sergeant came onto the unit and went absolutely berserk at me for being out of my cell. He was frothing at the mouth and screaming at me, and I didn't even have time to tell him that I couldn't push my own button in the control room, or that it was shower day and I was next man out to shower. I thought I was out of my cell as dictated by my routine. Fuck that shit. I didn't have a chance to say a thing, when he grabbed me by the throat and pinned me up against the cage of the day room and choked the shit of me.

At first, I tried to stay passive, because he was so short that he couldn't get a great grip on my neck to begin with, and that just pissed him off more. As two of his officers rushed in to get some of what he was having, he grabbed me by the hair and flung me in the cell—with a kick to my back for good measure. I was really pissed off, because he had done this to me just because of a button being pushed too soon on the pod. What the fuck?

So, there I was, sitting on the bed, a bit shook up and really angry, while being "cackled on" and Bobby laughing at me having my hair pulled so hard. His pal, Dave, went to his door next to him, and was doing all that he could to keep his nose in Bobby's butt crack. He made it seem as if every one of Bobby's sarcastic comments about me getting choked on by Sgt. Rage was, oh, so clever and funny! The two of them loved the opportunity to feel so happy as a couple, and would cherish that moment for ever and ever . . .

I didn't bother with retorts, because I knew by the way everyone was acting that the shit would just escalate further and further. I wouldn't have to say anything for someone to be combative with me.

This is where things turned around for me, I think. That day, I told myself that if I couldn't get through being on this unit without being dragged down into the gutter-style brawls, then so be it. I had tried for so many years to be passive. And now, I had just let a little prick of a man choke me when I could have whipped his ass. It was so humiliating to know that you could best a man physically, but, because of his absolute power over you, you had to let him abuse you.

I decided I was going to only take so much shit before I finally let loose on someone, even though I just hated thinking of me telling my parents how I tossed away any hope we all had with a new set of criminal charges from that place.

I made my mind up that if all of these crazy bastards were feeling like it was time to do whatever they wanted to me, I wouldn't take much more of it from there on out.

It saddens me to think that, during that brief period, I had such dark thoughts. Remember, I was just told that all of the biological evidence from my Death Row murder conviction case had been destroyed, so I honestly believed that I was going to die there in that miserable hole.

Now, as much as I'd like to claim that I had it all planned out, the truth is that what happened from there, really unfolded because of what "others" mostly did to one another. I just kind of helped by making sure that it happened, I guess.

I was willing to do whatever I had to do to keep the other maniacal killers on my pod all aiming their scorn at one another. It was easy to manipulate most of them, because of how they were wired mentally.

The fact that I had studied forensic psychology helped me to identify many of the traits in these men, and I was then able to prey upon their weaknesses, or strengths, using that knowledge.

I closely observed the others living around me, with a mental perspective, for the simple purpose of survival my studies provided me. I learned to use my skills to charm, cajole, or bully them into being malleable partners in my unit. It was a lot of work at times, and there were some wasted cases, like Roland, with whom it was pointless to even try. But I worked at it day and night; it was my "thing," or my technique for living with those men.

A good thing for me personally was that the "size and history of violence" mattered. By that point, I had survived many battles with others. Because I was big enough to give them all they could handle, most men left me alone. Some of those past opponents had very big reputations as brawlers, too. Based alone upon my history of fighting them, the men then around me knew that I was not someone who would let anyone walk all over me.

That whole "guards on inmate shit" with Sgt. Rage gabbing me didn't count, because a man in prison had the right in other prisoners eyes to simply not want to give up his life over a "silly moment." No man wanted to have new charges keep him there forever, either. That was accepted to be strictly *his* business. Let another inmate try to do the things that a guard tried on you, and that was when you would have no choice but to act as if nothing mattered — and then hurt them.

Then, lucky for me, a series of events occurred in which my physical actions had very little to do with taking out two of my enemies at once. I liked how it all came about.

At Pittsburgh Penitentiary, Death Row inmates were taken for visits from a five-story building, across the compound, to the main visiting area.

There, they were put behind a ten-foot section within the main visiting room, enclosed in security glass. Inside, there were metal stools, with telephones mounted on one long counter. Behind the thick security glass were a series of five stools, with a phone above each stool.

As a Death Row inmate, you were brought into what looked like an aquarium of sorts for visitation. You were like an animal on exhibit for all the normal visitors and children to see, while seated inside that glass box.

Of course it was all built using inmate labor, and had the shoddiest set of phones possible for visitation use. All of the phones were connected to a security booth, hidden within the walls of the visiting room, and complete with a two-way mirror fitted on its door. A guard, hiding within the booth, listened in on the conversations on each phone.

The visitors room was the most awkward place to see your family, because all you heard were two, three, or even four inmates on your side of this big glass enclosure, as they shouted answers to unheard questions being asked of them over the phones. You had to work hard to try to blot it all out, and still be able to focus on what you heard on the tinny phone before you. Invariably, you found yourself shouting, too.

Lots of times, if it were just one or two guys at once on those phones inside the visiting room, it was easier to deal with. The only problem was that sometimes the guard in the hidden booth left ALL of the lines open, so anyone using a phone heard all the other conversations at once. This was annoying even at the best of times, and led to my having a bunch of shit to deal with on my unit later on.

It all started with Rump being pulled out for a visit. He was searched, got dressed, and left the unit with guards "Frick and Frack."

Oh, man, those were the two guards whose job was to float around the jail, taking men from our unit (or other disciplinary units under our floor at the top) out to visits, or to the hospital, or to court processing. They were two of the most "fuck with your mind" guys ever. Both were huge, white, and "wired-for-combat," which is how I described them. Push a panic button for help anywhere in the prison and those two guys lighted up like zoo animals who knew it was feeding time!

They did all sorts of random things to men. They would get you into that slow-ass elevator with them, and, on the way down, hit you with "body punches" to warm up their huge muscles.

"Frick and Frack," (they got their nicknames from both having the name "Frank," or somehow having Frank in it) were a bad combo to handle. Those guys even made up their own moniker of sorts, because they knew that made them more menacing in jail. If you saw one of those guys without the other, it seemed odd, and you waited for the other to show up. Together, they put on their "stage act" for the psychological effect alone it had on men. It was borderline sociopathic the way they fed off each other, committing heightened acts of "one upping" the other, involving the pain and torment of inmates.

I had no desire to be in their care at any time, but, one day, later on, I managed to make them both regret messing with me in a really fucked up way, all because of how they treated me.

But right then, I had to deal with "Frick and Frack" coming to take me out to a visit, right after Rump left. I knew, as soon as I heard I was being taken out, that I already had that loud-ass Rump to listen to over the phones while I was down there. I just hoped there wouldn't be any of the "shit tossers," from the mental ward beneath our unit, in there as well. They even took off their clothes, or touched themselves, while in the booth looking at females. Seriously, they had no reservations, nor did they feel anything about doing it.

Nothing made a visit suck worse than some guy who decided he saw a female who was just an innocent visitor, and was "hot enough" for him," in the general population visiting area. He would then whip out his dick and start masturbating while inside the secure area. It was really sad when you had to ask your mom, or someone else who had driven for hours and hours to come see you, to please go to the toilets, or to look away. You then got to watch while the guards rushed into the restricted visiting area and beat the guy with clubs, before dragging him off the counter on which he was standing. Then, they'd come back in with an inmate to wipe the semen off the visiting room glass.

When my pod opened and those two guards stood before my cell, I went through the same procedures in order for me to leave the unit. I handed over my clothes to be searched, then stood in clear view of both men and showed that neither my crotch nor my ass crack had anything hidden in them by spreading myself wide. I opened my mouth, so they could shine a huge light inside to make sure I was not taking any handcuff keys or small notes out of the unit in my mouth.

They handed my clothes back to me, and I correctly put on my undershorts, T-shirt, socks, orange jumpsuit, and finally my rubber-soled shoes. Once I was fully dressed, they put cuffs on me, while wearing rubber gloves, and put a tether on the cuffs, which one man held firmly as I exited my cell. Then they each grabbed an arm, and they led me off.

When I got on the elevator with the two men, I had to endure a nearly three- to five-minute, creaking ride down in that elevator. All the while, they munched on a bag of potato chips that they had taken off my desk inside my cell at the last minute. They treated themselves to this "gift" when my cell was "searched" following my being taken out for visit.

As we rode slowly down, they took turns crunching the chips loudly in my face, up close to my ear, or right in front of my eyes. After each mouthful, one man or the other stuck his huge hand into the bag and filled his mouth with another portion. Oh, they even burped in my face once or twice to share their smelly, potato chip breath—along with the aroma of whatever they each had for breakfast—all while smiling in my face. I stood there silently, and imagined that I was on a train platform, looking off into the sky and contemplating my day, as if nothing bothered me . . .

In my mind, though, I was thinking how those two jokers needed to be taken down a peg some day.

Now I don't want to segue too far from the trip on the elevator, going to my visit that day, but you have to know that if those dudes wanted to play with me—as if I were a "puppet"—then I was going to get back at them if I could. I had to make them respect me, and make them realize that I was not being a sap. But my turn at "having fun" with them would have to wait for another day, because I was on my way to see my spiritual adviser. She was hell bent on making me try to "behave" while I was in that place. If she only knew what she was asking of me . . .

Now "Frick and Frack" were not allowed to just vouch for my having been searched, and to put me in the visiting room. Instead, they had to hand me over to the visiting-area officers, so that they, too, could remove my chains and clothing. I was then strip searched all over again by the new officers, and put into "visiting" clothes that were a simply awful, plum-colored shirt and elastic, waist-banded trousers.

I was then put into a set of handcuffs, in front, which had the cuffs welded to a metal ring that was sewn into the front a three-inch-wide leather belt. The loose ends of the belt had a buckles on one end, and a tongue with holes in it on the other, with a small lock affixed to it that would be secured in the rear while I was wearing it. There was no way I could undo the belt, once it was locked.

Then I was taken into the huge aquarium-like visiting room, where only Rump sat alone by the end stool, farthest from the door.

I sat down on my stool and waited for my spiritual adviser to come through the visiting room and over to where she could sit in front of me on a metal stool. I looked sideways at Rump and his visitor. I picked up the phone just to check, and I could already hear them speaking, which meant that all of the lines were open. *Shit!*

Rump had gotten himself a "gal." He had a pen pal, who wrote him letters; she was a woman who was part of a local church group. To Rump, this was surely heaven. He got to have time out of his cell with a very big-breasted, mature lady, who was divorced and very sweet by nature. While out there in the visiting room, he would become all aroused, and did his best to be charming.

Then, he would go back to his cell, and furiously masturbate, while playing it all over in his mind.

Whenever he returned to his cell after a visit, we would hear him talking to her aloud, as if she were still present. He had cut a hole in his foam-filled mattress, and put her photo above it, so that it was at eye level when he lay on the mattress. He would put butter around the hole, stick his penis in it, and say he was "riding her." He proudly urged us all to listen to him, while he was showed us how he would handle her in bed if he got the chance.

To avoid thinking of my man doing a "cowboy impersonation" in his cell when he was in front of me in the visiting room, I tried to focus on anything that I could lock onto with my eyes. I did so, while trying not to trigger an attack from Rump, who was so unstable mentally. The guy was super strong when he flew into a rage, and I was *not* going to play with him while he had his "boo" right in front of him. If that poor woman only knew about his mattress antics . . .

So, I was trying to keep my shit together, as Rump whispered the worst sexy talk to his woman, over the phone. All I could think about was what in the world the guard hidden in the booth, behind the two-way glass, must be thinking about, listening to that guy talking his sexy talk.

Rump had his nose broken so many times in the past that it made a really awful noise when he breathed. I sat there waiting for my visitor, while thinking of how it must have been the worst job ever, to be in that two-way, mirrored booth, if Rump had a hard-on in his trousers. It had to be sickening to listen to his breathing, as he became all excited sexually while he talked to that overweight woman in the one-size-fits-most-dining-room-tables kind of dress that she wore.

I tried really hard to keep my silly ass mind from thinking about whether or not Rump mentioned his drinking habits to her, or the fact that he liked to sleep in bar toilets.

Finally, I saw my spiritual adviser coming over, and I smiled as though I was, at long last, seeing someone sane in the midst of that fucked up place. She sat down and looked at me with a really odd look on her face. I was wearing a look on my face that was a mix of "help me" and "you are not going to believe this shit."

Standing at the phone that day, I did that thing of casting my eyes to the right, and encouraging my visitor to take note of who we were sharing the phones with. I tried to get her to look over to where Rump sat, and then raised my eyebrows a bit.

My spiritual adviser, not being as careful as I was of letting things slip, was a bit too obvious in looking in that direction. While she did not recognize the man on my side of the glass partition as Rump, she, nevertheless, sure eyed his visitor up and down. She looked at me quizzically, and I did the whole "I wanna tell you, but I have an eight hundred pound Gorilla sitting beside me" look—the look that said: "This guy is liable to snap at any minute and beat me around the room like a piece of luggage, he if finds me mocking his girl."

So, like the stupid mother fucker that I was, I mouthed the number "81" to her. She looked at me like I had lost my mind. So, I made a second, and even stupider-looking try at mouthing the numbers "EIGHTY ONE!" Then I noticed people staring at me, while I was standing there holding a phone at my waist.

To visitors standing behind my spiritual adviser and looking in my direction, I must have appeared to be a man screaming loudly at her. I gave a shake to my head and finally gave up. I slumped down in my chair when I realized that I looked like a maniac who was loudly yelling "81" to my visitor, when, in fact, I was not making any sound at all.

At last, my spiritual adviser finally caught on to what I was saying. Her face lit up, as she recalled me previously telling her how Rump had an IQ of just 81. She sat bolt upright with her eyes bright, just as I realized that Rump would be able to hear her speaking into the phone!

As soon she understood what I had tried to do by pointing out who I was next to, I should have put my fingers to my lips right then. I should have made eye contact, and pleaded with her to keep her mouth shut, letting her know that I knew *she* understood the gag.

But just as I tried to shut her down, sure as shit, she said, "Oh, *that* 81!"

And just like that Rump's most embarrassing moment had been exposed. The easiest way to make you understand is to tell it like it happened . . .

It was three weeks earlier to the day, and I was hoping to God that Rump wasn't going to beat me like some bartender, when I witnessed the craziest post-visit moment by any prisoner. I could never had made this up.

First off, Rump is *literally* retarded. According to the law, you have to have an IQ of 79 or less to be spared execution. Rump was tested by the courts and it was determined that his IQ was 81. I knew this, because when he came back from his visit with his attorney, where he had learned of his IQ score, the boy was soooo happy.

He was on his door immediately, calling out to Dave that he had just gotten a "play." He explained that he was getting off Death Row because of his brain score!

When I heard that shit coming out of his mouth, I dropped the book that I was reading and got on the door along with everyone else. Any news of one of us getting out of there drew two immediate responses: anger and resentment—anger, because someone was getting out of there and you were not, and resentment, because of the things they started shouting at us like, "You dead mother fuckers *eating* it now!" They were those quaint, hurtful, parting shots they took at us as they walked out of hell, just to piss us off one last time.

So, just before I witnessed all those men get angry and wanting to see him dead, Rump went and told us all how he was getting off Death Row thanks to the wonderful "play" his lawyers had just gotten him from the courts.

Rump stood at his door and said the courts had a law that said anyone with a "79" was allowed out to be in population. The way he said the number "79," I wondered if anyone had bothered to tell him that it was his IQ score they were talking about.

Well, it was indeed his IQ score that he soon bitterly learned about. You see, Rump was nearly through telling us how he had about a year left with us on "the row," because his lawyers said they filed the appeal for the matter, when Bobby viciously attacked.

He started saying how stupid Rump to show us all what a lame brain he was, because he'd been given "two points" as a "pass" by the courts. Bobby went on to say how "lucky" Rump was, and that his IQ of a retard was well earned. He summed it up cruelly by saying that, technically, Rump was a moron. He then laid into Rump, saying how he was fuckin' brain dead anyway. Bobby totally humiliated him like that for a good five minutes.

Ever since that day, Rump had been gunning for Bobby. But that bastard was so huge that Rump wouldn't take him on *unless* he had a decent weapon. They both hated one another, yet still hung out together in day room, and did crazy shit like playing cards together.

Bobby was dominant over Rump in that "suck-up-to-the-beast (while hating the beast)" relationship they had together.

Back to the visiting room.

My visitor had just picked the giant scab off of my buddy Rump's IQ test debacle, and things went bad really quick. Rump stood up and glared poisonously at me with his best "you're gonna die, bitch" look, then dropped the phone on the counter top. In return, I gave him my own look that said, "What? I didn't do *shit?!*" But he was too pissed off to give me a pass.

I kept my eyes on him as he kicked on the door of the visiting room to be let out of there. When they got him out of the booth, I looked at my visitor and said, "Nice one. You know, now, I gotta go fuck him up for this, right?" She just shrugged, as if to say, "How could I know?"

So, after about an hour of the most awkward prison phone visiting time was over, I went back to the pod. On the ride up, Frick and Frack told me how Rump changed his mood with them on his return to the unit, and they wondered aloud "who" or "what" could have made him quit his visit early with his church-lady friend with the big tits . . .

They said it as though they half-expected me to give it all up to them, and join them laughing at Rump. But I wasn't about to feed them anything they could use on Rump that would give him new issues with me. I was too busy counting how many paid envelopes I had in my cell right then . . .

I knew Rump was going to come right after me; he was probably already back on the pod telling anyone who would listen how I had just fucked up his visiting time. But I bet he didn't mention it was related to his IQ "thingy." Yeah, I was probably back there telling the guys that I did some shit to mess with his visitors while they were there to see him.

When I got back on the pod it all had that "we just got done talking about this asshole" feel to it. I knew my name was being used, and I also knew that Rump was fuming angry. It was then that a new guy was put into Gary's old cell, one who'd be the bridge to my needs.

His name was "Yhati," and he was just a kid—real name was KenYata—a slender light skinned black guy who was all of about 20-or-so-years old. He was on Death Row for a simple drive-by shooting, the usual "hood" kind of crime. He had this over-the-top personality and was constantly hyperactive, so much so that he was placed in Pittsburgh because they felt he was "too wild" for a more open setting any place else in the state.

Yahti wouldn't last long. His death is still one big, fucked-up mystery. He was too frail for that place, I guess.

I liked Yahti personally, and we played chess together early on. I often joked with him about his "hood" life and how his game was much like that of a "crack head." I felt a bit of a kinship with him, because we both were basically children at that time of our lives when we were put on Death Row.

Other than his not wanting Roland to be his new sex partner (which he made clear right off to him), Yahti was "neutral" to everyone on our pod. He wasn't old enough to be "in the mix" very much yet. He was kind of an untouchable anyway, what with him being a member of the "Junior Black Mafia" of Philadelphia.

There were like four or five of the head members of that notorious gang scattered on Death Row, and they didn't let anyone mess with one of their foot soldiers. Yahti had checked on that.

So basically Yahti could play around with Bobby or any of the others verbally, all while knowing that none of them would kill him. He wise cracked his way along, each day, and no one better mess with him about it either.

Now I knew Yahti had just come back from time spent down in the county jail. That meant that he had a gut full of balloons with weed or coke in them. He "muled" regularly like that for the bosses in the gang, and that, too, gave him sway over others in the unit.

I figured that since Rump was broke, and I had a bunch of paid envelopes in my cell, I could get him "baited" enough to get him off me. I needed to get him to lose sight of wanting me dead from the visiting room incident, while I fed him someone else to focus his anger on.

So, I called over loudly to Yahti, and got him on his door to hear me. I said I had three hundred paid envelopes, and wondered "could he hook me up?"

Yahti told me he had me covered. It was then that Rump, hungry to get some weed out of it, called over to say that he would move it on his homemade string line, moving it from Yahti's cell over to mine. We really didn't *need* his help, but he was insinuating himself into the move like I wanted him to, so I let him. We agreed to let him pass the envelopes back to Yahti for us as well. I smiled, because I knew he wanted in so he could get something for his involvement.

Then, in a voice loud enough for anyone who Rump had been bitching to about me for my messing up his visit, I said, "Hey man, sorry about that shit downstairs. I told that bitch she wasn't cool for doing that on a visit!"

Rump chimed right in and agreed that "my visitor" was now the one who had fucked things up, and how he saw me as a pal again for apologizing to him.

I got more into "my role" then, saying he and I were still cool and that I really told that bitch who came to see me that she had to go! I even said that was why I came off my visit early, too, because I wanted to set things right out of respect for Rump.

Rump warmed up to what I was selling then, especially since he knew he was getting some of that weed from Yahti . . .

So, I sent the three hundred paid envelopes, which I placed in a small pretzel bag that was sealed inside two other bags, one within the other, and all attached to a string in front of my door at floor level. Then, I then sent it over so that Rump could snag it, and he flung it along the floor to Yahti.

The bag arrangement was always necessary, in case some rotten bastard in the cells between all of us took that moment to toss a cup of piss (or piss *and* feces mixed up in a cup) on the floor, in an effort to ruin your envelopes or other items.

Once Yahti was paid, he sent his line over with two grams or so of weed in it. Rump brought the balloon in and he waited. Then, and perfectly on cue, I said, "You take half of that now, Rump, and you can pay me back later."

We both knew he wasn't paying me shit for the weed. He was gonna take nearly all of it, too. He played his "retarded card" perfectly at times like that. He made a big show of sending me over the rest — *after* he had taken his share — just so everyone would know he hadn't ripped me off in a petty way.

I know it seems insane that he needed to do what he did to show everyone that he wasn't a total asshole to me, but that was the world I lived in.

After a while, I heard about six or seven flushes of the toilet in Rump's cell. He was taking a puff on a "one-hitter," which was a homemade pot-smoking pipe, all while standing over his toilet, so he could blow the smoke into the commode, then flush it to suck away the smoke.

By now, I was betting he was pretty fucked up. About five minutes later, Rump began making noises in his cell that were really strange. It was the "headphones-on-his-head while-singing" sounds that we soon heard.

They were weirder than those you usually heard when a Death Row prisoner like Ronnie, who was fucked out of his face on drugs, did it — especially when he was singing only half of the words to the songs he was listening to. It was all very passionately done, at an emotionally charged, high pitch, which made it sound so weird.

After a break in his performance, Rump got to sobbing as he sang, and he sometimes started crying over the words to the music. It was like some really messed up opera act shit, and you just wanted it all to stop. The fact that Rump loved county music made it all the more fucked up, because he was getting all emotional over some dog dying in the song . . .

You laughed if others were laughing (as I did then), but didn't want to be the one laughing when he took off the headphones and heard you saying shit about him.

That was exactly what Bobby was doing when he wondered aloud to Dave, "I wonder if Rump is crying because he was thinking about how he used to be the dog in that cage that had died in the song?" That was followed by, "Or, do you think it is because he wants to fuck that dog in the cage like he wants to do to his lady friend with the big tits, who comes see his sick ass on visits?"

That was exactly what Bobby had just finished yelling (a bit too loudly) to Dave, when Rump went from singing his heart out, to flat out screaming at Bobby in response to hearing his taunts.

Oops. I guess Bobby did fall for my set-up.

I shoved my face into my pillow, while laughing hysterically, as Bobby rose to the bait from Rump. He and Rump went to work on each other about mothers with farm animals, including all manner of shit being said about one another's family members.

Things got heated up pretty quickly after that first round of insults about each other having "whores," or "faggots" for parents. Then, they escalated things further by making it known that, as soon as the doors popped open again, it was going to be "World War III, bitches!"

When I saw that Rump and Bobby were going to go at it physically, I immediately leaped into the fray. I took

Rump's side by getting on my door and shouting at Bobby, too. I shouted that Bobby was nothing but a "big fat bitch," adding that Dave was his "old lady" in prison, and how Dave loved to suck Bobby's ass every chance that *she* got.

That got both Bobby and Dave into it, and I smiled slyly as I set the stage for what I wanted to happen next. I kept pumping up Rump by saying things like "Fuck 'em Rump, they're just jealous because you and me got down smoking Yahti's good shit!"

Rump kept at it until we got bored after twenty minutes, and all settled down for the weekend.

You could smell the hate simmering and seething inside of that place for the next two days. I made sure I laughed coarsely a whole lot that weekend, too, just to keep them angry at what I found so funny.

Sunday night, Bobby helped when he came to the door, remembering something that he'd forgotten earlier during the shouting match on Friday . . .

Out of nowhere, about nine o'clock on Sunday night, Bobby started calling Rump "Captain Pooh," over and over in a sing-song voice. That was when I knew there would be a bloodbath on Monday morning. I knew things were for real when day room finally arrived, and Bobby started to really humiliate Rump.

Poor Rump. He was asked to bring back a dozen or so balloons once, after a trip he had taken to the main prison. It had been arranged by others in "gen pop," and all he had to do was follow instructions. He agreed to pick up the balloons at the hospital during a post-op, check-up following his hernia surgery. Once an inmate passed them to him, all he had to do was swallow them, come back to his cell, and crap them out.

However, Rump, being the foolish person that he was, told us all that he had a package inside his guts that he wanted removed just as soon as he was back on the pod, after he returned from the hospital that evening.

All night, he talked bout how he couldn't wait to shit those balloons, so he could get high. Dave told him that if he was so anxious to unload them, he should try using enemas to help him shit.

In typical retard fashion, Rump said that he had enough enemies, and we all laughed at his dumb ass for misunderstanding Dave. Then Dave told him that he would make "something" that Rump could use to get the drugs out, and that he should ignore us dicks for laughing. We all waited to see what would slide out of Dave's cell for Rump to . . .

So, out came a half-squashed shampoo bottle that appeared to have an ink pen stuffed into the spout opening. I could see that it had some white string holding it securely to the top of the bottle. I surmised that this object was going to be filled with water and shoved up Rump's ass, in an effort to somehow try to flush out his intestines.

It was nearly 10:00 p.m., and we were due for a guard shift change, so he should have just chilled. There would be a time when the only guard on duty would make his lone pass on the unit to see if all forty-eight of his "children" were in their cells. With his one chore done, the guard usually went to sleep in the control booth for eight hours. Rump could have waited another ten minutes or so, but "retards" don't have normal brains that permit them to do the obvious things that others do. So, when the pod doors kicked open, that fucking idiot was on his knees inside his cell with an ink pen shoved up his ass (which was attached to a bottle filled with a quart of water).

Now, we all knew that Rump was doing that shit inside his cell, so of course Bobby tried to stop the guard and talk to him about some request slips he said he needed. The guard ignored Bobby, slammed the outer door on the first side of the pod, and kept right on walking . . .

He was ten steps along when we all heard, "WHAT THE MOTHER FUCK ARE YOU *DOING* INMATE?!"

The passing guard observed Rump on all fours with the bottle sticking out of his ass, with one hand holding the bottle, while using his other hand to try and squirt water up into his ass. That was when the guard loudly yelled what he did for all of us to hear. Of course, in a panic, Rump snapped the pen off in his asshole, as he tried to yank it out.

He screamed in agony at his ass being ripped apart. He kept yelling that his ass was bleeding, and the guard broke into hysterical laughter as he pulled out his walkie-talkie to call for other guards in the unit. He shouted for them to get up there on his floor right then.

He poured it on, too, shouting over the PA system that he had just found a guy jamming a bottle up his asshole!

On the pod, we all laughed so hard because they had to put Rump on a gurney and roll him out to the same hospital he had just come from—only *now* it was to get a pen out of his rectum. Of course, they also removed the drugs from his stomach—once they figured out what he had been doing in his cell. They put Rump in a sealed room for a week, with nothing in it but a bucket.

Rump told us later how he broke the stitches that were in his asshole, bragging that, despite all the nasty mess, he even tried to break open a shitty, blood-soaked balloon, so he could eat some of the dope before they took it all from him.

Rump was dedicated like that I guess . . .

I knew that night, after Bobby called Rump names to remind him of the hospital incident, how either he or Rump was probably dying on Monday morning.

I even bought Rump half a bag of hooch from George, the guy who bartered for everyone's fruit, all just to make wine from that material inside his cell. George would starve himself by trading all his food away for a few apples here, or a half-finished grapefruit there, all so that he could drink hooch.

I knew that George always had a batch of hooch cooking, and I figured that since Rump was definitely going to lose against that giant, why not buy the man one last drink on a Sunday night? I even sent over the last of the weed from Yahti, so Rump could sing all night long and really piss off Bobby even more.

What no one else but Bobby knew then, was that I was working on Rump in the vents between our cells the whole time. I told him that we should just take Bobby out together on Monday when we both went to the day room as a team. I said I had a nice weapon that I was gonna use on Bobby to help finally get things over with. (I lied of course.)

I told Rump that I also had a metal lock left over from my cell property locker, and that I managed to sneak it back to my cell from the property room when we first came into the pods. I said I had put the metal lock into two pairs of socks, tying them tightly around it to make it into a "lock-in-a-sock" weapon. I said he could bash in Bobby's brains with that thing, while I stabbed Bobby to death with my prison "shank."

I guess Rump was all excited to finally have someone help him murder humans now, since, in the past, he had to do it all by himself. He kept saying "yeah," over and over, each time I told him how big and sturdy the shank was that I had made for us to use.

So, I sent the "lock in the socks" to Rump late Sunday night, slipping it discreetly to him on a line that I had made. Then, I made sure to pump him up some more with a note I included with the lock, which read: "Bobby sucks dick!"

I knew I couldn't risk using big words in the note I had written to Rump, so I stuck to the ones that I knew Rump understood easily. I heard him say "Yeah!" one more time after he read my comment about Bobby's oral skills. Then, I went over and lay in my bed while waiting for the morning's excitement to begin. It was like anticipating the most fucked-up Christmas morning ever.

Finally, Monday morning arrived, and the execution of my little stage play went like so:

First, the sergeant came around and opened all the slots and took the names of those who were going out to the yard or day room for exercise.

Bobby was ever so eager to sign up for day room, making sure that Rump heard him say it very loudly. That was the challenge.

Rump waited until Dave said he was going to the yard next. I thought that maybe because Dave was so deeply tied to big Bobby, he reacted emotionally whenever his man was involved in a fight like that. Dave got very upset whenever that happened (like any wife would), and they were watching their partner stab a fellow human right before them.

Then, Rump said, in his best cowboy voice ever, "Yup, I'm going to the day-room, too!"

Sgt. Rage did not catch on to the challenge between Rump and Bobby, so he just moved on. I was next, and, of course, said that I was going to day room as well.

Hearing me say that, I knew that Rump was all pumped up (he knocked ever so softly on my cell wall, letting me know he had heard me sign up for day room). He must have thought that clearly we were a team, up against "Mr. Big Bad Bobby." Everything was now set to kick off in about an hour's time . . .

Then along came Poor George, who *had* to go and sign up for day room on that go round. No one else on that side wanted day room but him. *Idiot.*

I was thinking that he really chose a bad day to come out and try to get on the phone. I mean, that was clearly going to be a kill zone, so what was he thinking when he did that?! I actually meant to send him a note to tell him to skip the day room that morning, but I forgot. Alright?

Now I know that I let that poor, crippled, brain-damaged man go right in there that day, even though I knew what was coming. I am not proud of that. I'm sorry, but that was not my main focus at that moment.

I actually needed George to at least *sign up* for the day room, so that they would start at Bobby's cell and finish with George being pulled out slowly in his wheel chair. The rest, I told myself, was on him for going out of his cell.

The guard in the control booth popped open the pod doors, right on time at 9:00 a.m. The guards entered the pod and went from right to left, taking Bobby to day room first. He sat at the table, far back from the door, with a deck of cards in his hands. Then Rump went in to join Bobby in day room.

When the guards got to my door, I yelled out that I was "on the toilet!" I told them to pass me over, because my stomach was bothering me.

Then, they picked George out of his cell. Once he was done going into the day room, the guards left our pod, so they could go around to the other pod next to ours, and get that one other guy needed to fill the four slots for day room time. That was my chance.

Rump stood facing my cell, looking at me for an answer as to why I let him go into the day room alone with Bobby. Clearly we were not doing this as "Team USA."

I ignored all that and kept mouthing the words, "Get him!" in response to his stares. I was looking out of my door at Rump, all the while making mean faces at him to spur him on to take action.

Bobby was sitting at the table with the deck of cards in his hands, shuffling them slowing. He was watching Rump from behind, as he stood facing me. I watched as George asked if Bobby minded if he used the phone. Bobby waived his hand at George, as though granting passage to a peasant his passage. So, Georgie-boy nervously backed his wheelchair toward the phone, all the while keeping his eyes on Bobby, unsure at that time, whether it was a joke or not . . .

As George wheeled himself backwards toward the phone, I nodded at him, and Rump chose that moment to strike. Facing me, he stuck his right hand inside his jumpsuit to fish out his weapon. He wrapped the athletic socks around his fist. Then he began pulling the "lock-in-a-sock" weapon out of his clothes. It was like watching a big, white, floppy worm come out of his belly.

He looked at me one last time (with that "here goes *nothing*" look on his face), then spun, without warning, while swinging the weapon at Bobby's face. Rump cracked Bobby square on the top of his head with the lock wrapped up in a pair of socks just as hard as he could.

Then, blood shot all over the day-room glass behind Bobby, and blood also began to run down Bobby's face from a gash about four inches wide, where he'd been cracked on the head with the metal lock. Rump swung again and again, as he cracked Bobby right on top of his head two more times with that thing.

Bobby rose up slowly out of his chair, shaking off the first blows from the attack. As he did so, he pulled out a big-ass, homemade shank from within his jumpsuit. He wobbled backwards, as Rump made a huge, arching swing attempt that missed. Instead of hitting Bobby with the wild swing, he shattered the window of the pod security glass with his weapon.

The lock ripped out of the socks Rump was holding, and went through the glass, only to fall onto the floor, outside in the hallway. Rump was left to stare at this now useless pair of empty socks wrapped on his hand after he missed. That was just as Bobby took Rump by the throat with his giant fist, pinned him against the mesh wire of the day-room walls, and began stabbing him.

Bobby stabbed Rump over and over in the belly, while holding him there like a rag doll. I know I saw him stab Rump in the belly at least twenty or thirty times, and yet Rump was still standing upright. He was fighting to get free of that fist, which was locked around his throat, as the guards came on the pod and sprayed both guys in the face with tear gas. They then entered the day room, and beat them both to the floor, while they cuffed each one with their hands behind their backs.

During the scuffle, George had been knocked over in his wheelchair, and Bobby even stepped on him once, as he tried to drag himself clear of the brawl. It was all over in a total of about three minutes. And, with the tear gas making everyone instantly sick, it was so chaotic that it was like we all had gotten involved.

It just went on and on, as they dragged Bobby out of day room, all the while clubbing the shit out of him, before they tossed him into his cell. Then, they came back into the day room, and began dragging Rump out by the feet, thumping him hard, too, for his part in what had just happened. As they dragged him past my cell, I saw just how he had survived those twenty to thirty stabbing attempts: He had magazines taped to his body!

I thought he had looked a bit chunky that day. Lucky bastard had taped all these fishing magazines around his body, using them like body armor to stop a blade. That's why he wasn't butchered by that shank Bobby had held in his giant fist and used on him.

The only guy on the pod who had fishing magazines sent to him every week was Dave. Don't ask me why a guy like Dave would do that to Bobby, loaning Rump his favorite fishing mags to protect himself in battle. I just believed what I saw on Rump's body. I knew damn well that Rump was too dim to make body armor for himself.

(So Dave, you hated having to suck up to Bobby all along it seemed. I feel ya, sir, I feel ya . . .)

I stood at my cell door and laughed and laughed at how I had just gotten two of the sickest monsters to battle it out for me. How clever I thought myself to have them do my bidding against one another like that. And all the while I stupidly laughed, there was one person who heard it all play out, who figured out exactly what I'd done to both Bobby and Rump — Roland, of course. And now, he was going to move on me for it.

As I stood there enjoying my moment of triumph, he decided to give me a taste of how it felt to be manipulated by the master himself. Now, he knew exactly how to do me in. I figured he had grown tired of waiting to get me himself, and I had just shown him a game he'd really like to try on me.

In the aftermath of their battle, Bobby and Rump received ninety days of disciplinary time each. They had all of their possessions taken away, and Rump was moved from of his cell into another one, which was away from all of us. (He was soon taken off Death Row because of his mental retardation, and put into "gen-pop," where he was to serve his sentence of natural life.)

I went back to handling my own problems, sitting in my cell and waiting for one of the others to try to kill me. It was business as usual after that fight. All they did was shuffle a guy or two around, and wait for things to settle down just a bit before they thought of something new for us.

6

How I became Prey

Three times a week I put myself at risk by showering on the pod in the area known as "shower room," which was the one enclosure that had a shower curtain in front of it, hung on a wire. Due to my nearsightedness, I always wore eyeglasses. As a result, I was truly vulnerable when I washed my hair, because I couldn't see without them. It was very nerve wracking, and you had to have "big balls" to be able to ignore everything else, and to do that without showing fear. I always wore shower shoes that had a good grip, and I never took off my boxer shorts while washing my body. I washed while wearing them.

I always shaved in the shower and not my cell. Because, without my glasses on, there was no point in trying to shave while looking at the blurred image reflected in the metal security mirror. So, I learned to shave in the shower with my eyes closed, using my hand as a guide on my face. (After many years of doing that, I can shave perfectly without once seeing my face.)

The guard who hated me the most was was an ex-cop who had gotten himself fired for being a drunk. He was a nasty piece of work of Irish and mixed European descent, with gray hair and a squat body, who stood about six foot tall. He was thick-waisted, with the body of a drunkard: a distended belly and a bowed back. He was loud and nasty tongued when he spoke to you, and thought nothing of getting on the intercom and reading guys' criminal cases aloud for the whole pod to hear. He would cut the phone off to your mom when he felt like it, and burn mail that you had waited for weeks to arrive. He just loved to fuck with guys' minds.

I didn't know it at the time, but Roland had made a new pal of that guard, and was working him good behind my back. They laughed at jokes together, and, for whatever reason, Roland soon got extra, law library time each week, so that he could go have sex with our new pod mate.

"Marty" was the name of the madman who'd been chosen to replace Rump on our pod. The guy was a little dark-haired maniac, who was about five foot five inches tall and weighed no more than a hundred and ten pounds. He was a "white boy" psycho who had, along with another guy, gone into a bank near his home town in a central part of Pennsylvania, and started massacring everyone inside on the spot.

Marty was deeply saddened that his co-defendant (and also his lover at the time) had turned state's evidence against him. They said he went "dark," mentally, after being betrayed at trial by his co-defendant, and having his heart broken.

Marty was as crazy as anyone I'd ever met, and loved to think that he was somehow not one of us "regular guys" on Death Row. He was full of "America is the land of greatness" in the speeches he made in his cell, while being hated and scheduled for execution by the same blessed country. Marty's thinking was so twisted that when Democrat Bill Clinton was elected as President — Marty was a staunch Republican — he went "mental" in his cell and said that no "Democrat" had the right to execute *him*!

And so it went, on and on. Roland was "living it up," all because he had gotten really good at sucking up to that one guard. As a result, he was able to have his new lover, Marty, leave his cell and join him for "romantic times" in the law library several times a week, and I couldn't have cared less.

But, all of that had an effect on me.

Roland was regularly visiting the sergeant's office and feeding them intelligence about who was doing what on our pod.

Of course, in the beginning, that snake fed them the truth, but then he'd spread whatever lies were necessary to the guards, to have them mess up anyone who he hated.

If Roland knew of anything that was going on inside the pod, the guards soon learned of it. One of the worst tricks he played on me was getting the guards to search my cell when he saw me get a package from a guy named "Lonnie." That "snitch-move" of his got me sixty days without my TV and radio, and I wasn't allowed any books to read for two months. That was a really dreary period of time.

But what really hurt me was that one shitty act that got my friend, Lonnie, killed.

It was some strange shit, but it's all there in the newspapers for you to read, if you want the truth.

Lonnie, whom everyone called "Jihad," was from West Philly. A light-skinned, easy-smiling kind of guy, he was sent to Death Row back in 1984. I met Lonnie in Holmesburg Prison, back in Philly, while I was down there for a court appearance. For some reason, he and I got along right from the beginning. Two years later, when I saw he had landed beside me on Death Row in Huntingdon Prison, I agreed to help him with his legal work.

With me and another guy helping him, Lonnie managed to get his death sentence commuted, and, instead, was given a sentence of life without parole for the robbery-homicide of a store owner.

Because I helped Lonnie back then, while he was on Death Row, he was always a loyal friend for what I did for him. While he was in general population at Huntingdon, he used to send me a dozen donuts each month from his "lifer's package." That was a prison privilege he had, which allowed him to buy outside food since he was in the Pennsylvania "lifers program." I made good money off that treat each month, and he kept me afloat like that for a few years while I was there. Then Lonnie was moved to Pittsburgh, and I lost contact with him.

One day, in 1996, I got word from Lonnie that he was recently back from court, and that he had heard I was in the security unit. He had been doing time with one of my friends named Norman who told Lonnie that I had been shipped to Pittsburgh the year before. Lonnie wanted to know if I was "okay" mentally, or if he could do anything for me. That message being passed was his way of staying true to the ones with whom he had bonded over the years.

The message from Lonnie was given to me by one of the "gen-pop" prisoners who came up each week to cut hair for the security unit prisoners. This job was fought for and given to only those guys who had serious pedigrees—and *not* by the staff mind you. You couldn't even apply for this job, because it was off limits to any guy in jail who not seriously connected. Why? Because so many important messages were sent by them, either verbally or in writing, to the leaders of gangs who were serving disciplinary time in the "hole," or those who were on Death Row.

When I heard that Lonnie and I were in the same jail, I sent him a message asking him to send me a package of whatever he could spare. I needed something that I could make money on then, since I lost all of my "hustles" at Huntingdon. He knew that I had quit getting high years ago, but had no qualms about making money from selling cosmetics and food, or especially postage-paid envelopes.

The only thing was, I had to go out and get it. That meant that I had to set up a trip to the hospital, which, in and of itself, was very hard for me to do, because I had already escaped prison once.

The only thing that I could do then was come up with internal bleeding or severe stomach issues to get out of my cell. I had to contrive the symptoms of some form of an internal injury, and use them correctly to be taken out to the Hospital to meet Lonnie.

I waited a week after I received the message from Lonnie before I sent word to him to be ready about the last weekend of that same month. Then, I got everything ready, in order to be transferred to the hospital (and did so in a way that no one wanted to physically handle me).

I purchased four bags of gum drops and six bags of BBQ potato chips from the commissary a week before I put my plan to work. I began to starve myself on a Monday, hoping that by Thursday evening of that same week, I would be ready to be taken out of that cell and over to the hospital.

On Wednesday of that week, I went to the shower and used a razor to cut myself just above the ankle of my right leg by moving the safety razor sideways on my skin until a good deal of blood came out. Then, I put a washcloth on it, and soaked up the blood without letting it get too diluted in the shower.

When I had a lot of blood on the cloth, I folded up the bloody wash rag and put it into the clear plastic soap dish that I had with me. I did my best to get more blood into the dish with the cloth by scraping my leg with the edge of the soap dish before I closed it.

Once I had a nice amount of my own blood stashed away, I washed off my leg, put on a pair of white socks, and stepped into my shower shoes, and went back into my cell, where I did my best to make sure the cuts healed by not moving much.

On Thursday morning, I began eating the gum drops and BBQ chips at the same time. As hungry as I was, it did not make that mix of gooey candy melting over sour BBQ chips taste any less awful.

There I sat with a plastic cup of water, eating gum drops and BBQ potato chips for an hour. I ate every last one of those nasty things, and went to sleep right afterward to let it all ferment in my guts overnight.

On Friday morning, I told Sgt. Rage that I was too sick to eat, and that I had blood in my urine. When he tried to talk to me at my door during head count, I told him I was unable to focus, and stumbled back to bed. I told him to come into my cell and look at my toilet, and while he did, I acted as though I might faint. He demanded that I back up to the door to be cuffed, while he called for my door to be opened. Once another officer had come over to be with him, he went into my cell.

I was holding up Sgt. Rage's yard and day-room sign-ups, and he said there had better be real blood in the toilet, or else my face would be bleeding if there wasn't any.

When he came into the cell, he saw the red droplets of blood on my white boxer shorts, right below my penis. He saw the blood on the toilet that I had let drip from the soap dish and onto the rim of the bowl to make it look real. Then he looked down into the bowl and saw all that blood and urine mixed together. He said to the officer, "Get this idiot to the hospital. This fucker is dying or *some* shit!"

I put my best "Oh, shit this is *bad!*" look on my face, then went over gingerly and sat down slowly on the bed with the guard holding my arm.

Ten minutes later, I was in the loving embrace of Frick and Frack. They were *not* happy to be moving me that early in the morning, before day-room time, before they'd even enjoyed their first cup of coffee.

I really put on a show for Frick and Frack, because, by then, I was wearing only boxer shorts. I handed all my clothes to them, groaning like a sad ghost. While I was doing that, I forced myself to fart as much as I could. The stench from the BBQ chips and gum drops was putrid and nasty, and was soon wafting out of my cell. The smell was certainly making me sick, so I knew that Frick and Frack had to be totally disgusted.

They tossed my clothes at me, got my door opened, and yanked me out in a flash. I kept acting all weak in the knees, hunching over in made-up pain, and moaning to them that I couldn't hold it any longer . . .

The whole time I was acting like that, internally I was trying my best to shit my pants. By the time our slow procession reached the elevator, I was letting out a steady stream of the worst gas ever from my ass.

They put me against the wall and told me that if I *did* shit myself on the elevator, they were going to fuck me up good. I pleaded with them that I was really sick, and was really messed up with blood in my urine. I said I couldn't help it. I even tried to make myself cry by thinking about Roland out there in the woods beating my mother to death — *instead* of one of those old ladies he had killed.

When the elevator reached the top floor, and the doors finally opened, we all got on together. They pushed me to the back of the car, holding me there with their clubs. They held me there, and as far away from them as possible, as they stood by the doors with their free arms folded over their noses, like train robbers hiding their faces.

I strained my guts as hard as I could at that point, and, sure enough, diarrhea came rushing out. It felt all nasty and warm, as it began to run down my legs . . .

Both guards were getting physically ill from the stench, and I kept trying to fart, or shit myself, over and over, as best I could, in order to make it worse for them, too. That went on and on in that slow moving elevator.

By now, Frick and Frack were cursing me through their shirtsleeves, their arms held over their mouths the whole time. They were like frantic men, who were dying from their own breaths, as that elevator slowly made its way down at a snail's pace. I never once broke character, and did my best to keep it together, knowing full well that, if discovered, that kind of trick got your brains beaten in. It was out-on-a-limb shit there, folks, and you didn't fool around about stuff like that, because, to them it was no joke.

Frick and Frack jumped out of the elevator minutes after we had all gotten into it, angrily spitting and gasping for air as they got off.

Then, after they had sucked in enough fresh air to clear out the nastiness, they turned back and grabbed the tether on my handcuffs, pulling me out violently by tugging on it. I nearly fell at their feet then, and they were so horrified that I might get shit on them if I touched them that they eased up a bit and let me get my feet under me.

Then, together, we took the nastiest walk I'd ever taken in my life, trekking off across the prison grounds to the hospital, while shit ran down my legs the whole time.

They swore at me the whole way, saying that if I didn't die from whatever was in my guts that smelled like that, they were going to make me wish that I *had* died from it—especially if *any* of *my* shit got on either one of them in the process.

I was taken to the shower rooms that were located inside the hospital wing, and allowed to strip alone in the shower, since no one wanted to come near me because of the smell. I put everything I'd been wearing in a pile as instructed and placed my clothes in the garbage bag I was given. I was issued new prison garments from the hospital ward instead of orange security ones, and also given paper slippers, since my shoes were ruined from the shit.

I was put in a secured room in what was then known as the surgery ward, and handcuffed to the bed by one arm. I could *not* get the smell of my BBQ potato chip shit-fest off me, nor could I get image out of my mind of what it felt like to be covered in filth, and yet still made to walk. It was like someone had burned a child's diaper full of shit, combined with take out Indian food all mashed up inside of it. All I can say is that my nose burned from the spicy-turd smell of it all.

In time, I received a brief checkup from the nurse on duty, who said that the doctor would be around after a while to examine me. I told her I was feeling a lot better, but I was exhausted and needed to sleep if I could. She said that she would let them know about that and that she would have the doctor come by later on when I was feeling better. The guard then un-cuffed me from the bed, as per her orders, and I rolled over and went to sleep.

All I had to do was wait it out in bed, until well past 3:00 p.m., when Frick and Frack left for the day, and I would be left there in the hospital for the whole weekend. Now, all I had to do was wait for Lonnie to show up . . .

I managed to get through the doctor's 2:00 p.m. call by again making sure to fart as much as I could in the room before he entered. I knew it was disgusting, but I *had* to convince them that I had a serious intestinal virus, or some internal injury, or ailment that would allow me to stay. Again, right away, I sensed that one wanted to breathe the nasty smell I was emitting, because the doctor stood at the door with a surgeon's mask held to his face, as he spoke to me about my symptoms.

I described perfectly all the symptoms of gastritis, or what could be a serious stomach virus. The doctor asked me if I had eaten anything that might have disagreed with me, but I told him that I had not eaten in days, because of the pain in my stomach. He looked at my unit notes and saw in my prison records that the staff reported I had not eaten since Monday. *Boom!* Job done. He said the blood in my urine was due to dehydration.

After telling me he was prescribing medication to help with what he surely though was a stomach virus, the doctor closed the door as quickly as he could. Then, he signaled to the officer, and the nurse with him, to note that I would be kept there for observation.

I smiled just a bit then, because I had done everything perfectly. I had gotten myself out of the unit, and I my boy Lonnie was coming over there that Saturday to see me. Lonnie actually worked as an orderly, right there at the hospital at the time, so it was going to be real easy. Then, all I had to do after we met was to make it back onto my housing unit without being searched by Frick and Frack.

Lonnie showed up Saturday morning, and I was at my door, smiling at him through the opening, proud of myself for getting so far along with my plan. He said he would be back after breakfast to "run things down" for me, but I didn't know if I liked hearing that, since it suddenly sounded a little fishy to me.

When I looked at him like I was just there to pick up his package, Lonnie reassured me by saying, "It's cool. You just gotta help a brother out." All I could think then was, *Oh, no. He did* not *just do this shit to me, after all did to get here . . .*

I ate my first food in days that morning, and, afterward, my sore belly kept beating up on me for what I did to it with the gum drops and potato chips. I felt so awful from the gluten and sugar that I had consumed that my joints ached. I also felt really slow-witted.

Lonnie came by that afternoon to collect the trays, and to clean up the floor. As he stood by my cell holding his mop, with me crouched down to look out of my pie hole, he told me that he had a treat in store for me. I asked what was on the menu, and he said, "Oh, the usual, but something *nice*, too."

Then I knew for sure that we had gone from Lonnie was going to "hook me up" (whereby we were both just going to have another moment of "bros" looking out for each other), to this new game of his.

I waited for Lonnie to show his hand.

"So, listen Nicky-boy," he began, followed by, "I got you *right,* but I need a favor, too." (There it was, the "Lonnie pitch," and I knew he was going to get me into some shit when next he spoke.)

Not wanting to tell me he had decided to actually *use* me, Lonnie said, nevertheless, he would *have* to use me for coming down there to the hospital. It was just like him to make a nice bit of money off me, while pretending that he had something for me. He said that since I was willing to come down there anyway, what difference did it make who made money? You can imagine the expression on my face when I heard t*hat* shit.

I looked at him the same way anyone would when he was just handed the real item he thought he was buying. There he was using me to take shit back inside the unit, most likely for the "Junior Black Mafia."

In reality, though, I soon learned that it was for one of Lonnie's prison pals housed in the unit below mine, someone whom he owed money to. He quickly forgot all about what he previously said about everything being all set up for *me*. And now he was telling me how he nevertheless was "hooking me up" somehow.

Yeah, right, Lonnie.

So, basically, whatever I was being "given" at the start of all this jailhouse bullshit was now my "risk/reward" for taking things back to the pod for him. I knew that what he was asking me to do could get me into serious trouble on the unit, or even result in new criminal charges. I looked at him a long moment and said, "Wow, *really*, Jihad?"

He replied, "Oh, come on, motherfucker, you act like you never did any *moves* before!" That was meant to remind me that I once previously ran a gambling operation, and that I used to sell schoolwork to "gen-pop" guys who were too dumb to read, let alone pass college exams.

None of that had anything to do with Lonnie setting me up to take back to the unit with me whatever he was making money off of. The way he was putting pressure on me, I knew he was deeply in debt to somebody, so I cut him a break and said, "Okay, road dog, what we gotta do *this* time?" I was told he had a "belly pack" for me to take back.

Oh, shit.

If you melted plastic around items, the plastic molded them all tightly together. You took a yellow, bin-liner bag and melted it around several objects, then pressed them down to conform to your belly's shape by standing on them for hours. You tried to make it crescent-shaped so that it would be mostly flat and moldable to your midriff.

Whatever was going to be in Lonnie's belly pack must have been worth a lot of trouble, because you hardly ever got anything big into the unit. All I could hope was that there were no saw blades, handcuff keys, or shank blades for making weapons of any kind inside that thing. Those would all result in new charges against me. Otherwise, there was either going to be a small amount of grass, along with some notes for the top guys in the JBM, and possibly some cash, too, inside of the thing.

My job was to get the package back to the unit and send it unopened to the top guy in the "JBM." He would break it down into who got what. I knew right then that I was going to get mostly screwed over, because once I let that package out of my hands like that, it was gone for good.

I knew that I wasn't getting the same respect from those guys that Lonnie had for me. I weighed my chances and thought about how I was being played in everyone's game. I just went along with it. Once I said that I was down with the plan, Lonnie brightened up. He told me he had to put things into play first, but that he had something "extra special" for me, just for doing that huge favor for him.

I could just imagine him coming back and saying some dumb shit about how I was gonna have to do some other dirty job, but he didn't pull a lame move on me like that.

I had one of the best Saturday evenings of my life that night! It was to be my only day to eat, because I had to get a concoction from Lonnie, Sunday morning, that I would take, which was meant to give me diarrhea again. There was no chance that I would have the same terrible gas during the trip back to my unit, because we didn't get any sweets, or BBQ chips in the hospital. I figured that I was probably deadly enough with my farts that weekend, no matter what, and all I had to do was take one more filthy, shit-encrusted walk back to my cell to be done.

7

Monsters and Madmen

Lonnie sent me over a Philly Cheese Steak sandwich from the kitchen that Saturday night, and he added some fruit cups as well. I was living it up good then, and even had some candy sent over on my dinner tray, to boot.

At ten o'clock that evening, the night officer came by and, without saying a word, left my pie hole open. I thought that was . . . well . . . odd, but kept my mouth shut. I was looking out of the pie hole of my hospital cell for, like, twenty minutes when a big ass shock hit me.

There was Lonnie with the nurse in tow, and it was none other than the nurse who was hooked up with the same lieutenant from our unit! I was so stunned that I just stood there like an idiot, as she reached into the cell through that pie hole and started trying to get my dick out of my jumpsuit in a hurry.

I was well aware that the nurses made good money doing things like that, but I had no idea how Lonnie got in on it with that woman. She fished around with her rubber-gloved hand and grabbed my cock.

I was hard in a matter of seconds, of course, but it was still a very awkward and embarrassing moment, and I lost it a bit when she ripped some pubic hairs out. She wasn't able to feel the hairs through the material of the gloves, and it all started to hurt then.

Suddenly, I wasn't enjoying any of it, but who the fuck says "no" to that kind of thing after years and years of being locked up? It lasted, like, maybe three minutes. I swear I had a death grip on the inside of the door, while that hand in the blue rubber glove gave me the most fucked-up hand job ever.

At one point, it actually got to where I was laughing at how stupid and dirty it all was, as I clung to the door, desperately hoping to not fall over. I admit that, despite all of that torment, I was aware that I had not been with a woman for eighteen years or so, up to and counting that very moment. I certainly wasn't going to let a little thing like having my pubic hairs pulled out ruin it all!

But it went really badly, as far as a sexual act went, and I felt really fucked in the head for days afterward.

I honestly do not think that if Busthead had bent me over, inside the day room, and forcibly eaten my asshole, I could have felt any less sexy.

I even closed up my own pie hole, and walked away from the door, after she wiped her blue glove on a hand towel before dropping it beside the bucket that Lonnie was standing next to.

Then, Lonnie came over to my door and spoke to me through the side of the door crack. He said, "Yo, Nigga, how you like *THAT* shit?!"

I said, "Man, that bitch ripped my shit up!"

He laughed his ass off, and as he was leaving said, "I guess you got all that white girl "pussy hair" on your dick, and *that's* what *your* problem is!"

I told him to suck my white girl pussy, and then to get off of the fuckin' floor. I tried to hold my shit together, and not to laugh, but it was useless.

My groin was burning from being roughly abused, and, despite how funny it all was, I managed to get past it all without letting it ruin my break from Death Row.

Sunday morning, Lonnie told me that he would be back that night with the "package" to take back to the unit. He said I better not fuck it up, or we were *both* done in that place. I just laid on my bunk wondering how in the fuck I always ended up in the craziest of shit. I laughed at how I ended up being the prize idiot in a game that was being played on me by guys who I did not really know.

And there I was, thinking that I was the one being clever by pulling the strings of others like Bobby and Rump in that place . . .

That Sunday night, I had a molded, plastic parcel, twelve inches long by eight inches wide, tossed through my pie hole. I was not at all happy with its size, and, judging from the feel of it, I knew it would be bad news if I got popped with it. I told Lonnie that he was a dick, and that if I ever got caught with it, and ever got off Death Row someday, I was gonna bust him in the head. I said it in the same way as though I was wishing him well on his journey.

In response, he told me to stop being a little bitch, and said that if the guys receiving the package in my unit didn't give me what was meant for me out of it, we would crack their heads together.

In other words, he was saying that I was on my own, and fuck it, at least he had gotten me a hand job from the nurse.

You had to love a guy who was so shrewd that he had you all along. Lonnie just tried to make you like him as a buddy—even after he had played you for a sucker.

One last item Lonnie gave me Sunday night was the plastic bag with four liquid laxative shots inside it. They were in individual two-ounce cups that were sealed shut like coffee creamers. If you drank one of those laxative shots, you were good to go. If you drank two, it was an all-day, sit-down on a shitty throne. You didn't go past two. I handed him back two of the cup packets and told him that he should have a toast with me. Lonnie grabbed his dick through his trousers and told me to "go fuck yourself, white boy." He handed me back one more of the cups, just in case my dumb ass spilled one. (I took all three, later, just to make sure.)

I miss that crazy bastard. He stuck to the code of being a "prisoner," and that's all that I can say about him. Lonnie was not an "inmate" who tried to be comfortable. He didn't play at being a "con" either. That's where you took on some bullshit "Bushido" warrior attitude to hurt others. No, he was a "prisoner," a guy who knew that he didn't belong there, but was willing to grow or master it all none the less.

Lonnie ignored what the "man" said you did to end up next to him in a cell. You were dealt with as fairly as anyone else. In that way, a con artist like Lonnie figured that you got what you deserved based on his evaluations. I had to respect Lonnie for the way did his time.

Now, I had to get back on the game, and to be sure to drink the laxative juice at about midnight. That way, I was ready to give my nasty performance by 8:00 a.m. I knew it was going to be a filthy job once again, and I hated to think that I would have to walk a long way, covered in my own shit, to pull off that stupid move. And I knew I was getting nothing out of it, either, so that was what made what I did that day all the more a total waste of time.

I could have been coy and left that shit to the end, the part about me getting nothing from the package, but that wasn't really important, especially when I think of how all my stupid efforts left Lonnie dead. But it also left me really prepared to deal with Roland over it.

So, I got the drinks down, and waited for morning.

Frick and Frack showed up about ten, and I had so much "real" pain in my guts, from trying to *not* shit myself, that I actually struggled to hand all of my clothes to them to be searched.

I had the package hidden by the toilet, and after I did my "I got nothing on me" strip dance (I actually almost shit myself while I was doing it), I secretly slid my foot over and snagged the parcel with it, sliding it with my foot to the door right below me.

I dropped my jumpsuit on the package when it was handed back to me, covering it from sight, then scooped it up off the floor, while letting out a steady stream of nasty farts.

I actually stuck the jumpsuit (now with the package hidden within its folds) back onto the pie hole for them a second time, and said to the guards, "WAIT! I GOTTA SHIT!" then, as loudly as I could, I shot a load of diarrhea out of my ass and into the toilet, complete with a lot of loud groaning.

Frick and Frack recoiled, standing well back from my door, holding their noses, while keeping me in sight. I finished, then painfully stood up, removed the jumpsuit from off the pie hole, and explained that I had been doing that every five minutes or so.

Then, I blanched like I was about to vomit next, and told them we had to hurry. While they stood at least five feet away (because of the stink I was emitting), I put my jumpsuit on and fitted the package to my belly. Using my hands, I made sure it was all smoothed down in front, before I stuck my hands out for cuffs.

All I had to do then was walk fifty yards to the hospital exit, then two hundred yards across the grounds of the prison to the elevator, and then another fifty yards back to my cell. Then it was over.

As soon as they got me belted, cuffed, and through the door of the hospital cell, I shit myself hard, one last time, before they touched me in the doorway.

I really didn't have to try hard to get that god-awful liquid and semi-hard substance to flow out of me with a gush. I felt the entire back of that white, prison hospital jumpsuit turning brown and wet from the waste that was running down my legs.

Frick and Frack pulled me through the hospital hallways as fast as they could, all while yelling for everyone to get the fuck out of their way. Then, they yanked me so hard across the prison complex that I nearly got hit by the food cart, which was coming out of the unit. When that happened, it nearly caused the package to come out of my waistband, where I had it tucked. By then, I was panic driven to make it.

For ten, nerve-wracking minutes, I had to keep right on shitting myself as I walked along, in order to keep it looking real. Because I'd taken way too much medication, I lost all control of my bowels. And, of course, the fear of being caught was not helping much either.

The whole back of my jumpsuit was literally soaked in feces, as I crab-scampered along with my two, fired-up escorts propelling me along.

My shit-soaked, paper, hospital shoes were falling apart, and one of them was drooping off my foot. I made a miserable effort to drag it along, to maintain a semblance of dignity, by at least wearing shoes, even though I was covered in shit.

The whole elevator floor was soaked with my feces. My "companions" on the ride with me said they were going me make me clean their boots with my tongue later. They were as angry as I had ever seen them. And yet, I was so close to laughing and/or pissing myself in fear that, honestly, I don't know how I ever got out of that elevator.

By the time the doors opened on the top floor, I just wanted the nightmare to be over, and I forgot all about the "hunched over because I am so sick" walk I'd been doing.

With my boys, Frick and Frack, yelling that the control officer better have my fucking door opened, "NOW!" I made a mad dash for the cell meant for me. They took my cuffs off, all the while trying to extend their arms as far away from me as possible.

As I began removing my jumpsuit, to start handing them my clothes, so they could search each item, they shouted for me to stop. Then my boy, Frick, walked over and kicked the pie hole on my door shut with his boot. Then, in unison, they told me to sit there in my cell, with all that stinking shit on me, and suffer like a dog.

They walked off the pod, and, with my heart pounding, I started to peel my jumpsuit off. The package was right there on the floor, because it had finally slid out and actually landed right there by my feet in the doorway. Had either guy just looked down at the floor, he would have seen that I had only half hidden it beneath my foot, the foot that had the shitty, paper shoe drooping off of it. Now, it stuck out like a squashed banana that was once in the center an ice cream sundae, which had been run over by a car on a muddy road.

When I looked at my foot, thinking of it that way, being a squashed sundae, I let go with a laugh like never before. It felt like I just let out all of that fear and disgust in one burst, for what I had done to myself and how it felt.

Once I got cleaned up, I put all my filthy clothes into a plastic bin bag the guards had brought me after Frick and Frack left. I cleaned up the package in my sink with soap and water before putting it inside two, potato chip bags, and sealing it with tape. Then, I slipped all of it into a bigger bag, which came off the loaves of bread that came into the unit on the food cart. I wrapped it all up in my filthy clothes, made it into a big nasty ball, and then pushed the intercom button, so they'd let me fling it out of my cell.

When I told the guard in the control booth that I had hospital clothes to be put outside of my cell, as they had ordered me to do, he told me to put them in the trash can that was located by the door of the pod exterior, and not to come fully out of the pod. He then remotely opened my door and one of the pod doors that had the trash can next to it at the same time. I put the package and clothes in the trash can, while Roland, in the first cell, watched. I could tell that he just knew I was up to something.

That trash can would be fished through by the worker on the unit who was there to clean floors after the last meals were served. He got the package out at some point and slid it to the guys on the pod where the JBM boys lived.

I got word from the worker, who tapped on the pod windows, letting me know it had gotten there safely.

By the time I received word, I had a shower and was in my cell, so I just lay there wondering if that would be the start of something else, with Roland telling the guards on me, or if I was just done with things.

I had to wait a day to see that Roland had indeed put two and two together. My cell was searched right along with the whole pod of cells on the other side of the unit where the package had been sent.

I was curious as to how only *my* cell on our pod was searched that day out of a whole pod of cells. The whole other pod, to which the package had gone, was stripped bare as well. I sat in my empty cell afterward, fuming because Sgt. Rage had taken all my belongings. I knew then that Roland had gotten all of us busted.

I was served with paperwork that said I had a balloon with a note in it, which was found in another man's cell, and that the note claimed that half of the contraband was mine.

Besides me, there were four men who came from the other pod, who all had their possessions taken from them for ninety days of disciplinary time. I watched Roland smirk at me in triumphant glee for days, as he passed by my cell.

So, what happened to Lonnie? you ask. He was brought to the disciplinary cells beneath the Death Row unit that I was housed on. During questioning by the guards, he had his teeth broken, but never told the staff who brought the drugs into the prison for him, so they could be sent to our unit. He got a year of disciplinary time in the hole for that.

Well, Lonnie was finally electrocuted in an "electric chair" in Pennsylvania (he had been sentenced to die back in 1984 by the courts). It was the craziest way anyone could have died, but the facts were there.

Lionel Baker, AKA "Lonnie," was electrocuted sitting on the toilet, inside of his cell in Pittsburgh Penitentiary. An inmate, with whom Lonnie shared his cell, broke open the wiring of a TV and, somehow, put the bare wires across the metal toilet seat. That crazy, wired-up toilet was now "live" and fully charged.

When Lonnie sat down on the toilet in his cell and urinated while sitting there, he closed the circuit on that death trap. His urine became the conductor of two hundred and twenty volts of electricity that coursed through his body, killing him instantly. They said his dick was even fried off. I couldn't imagine a more horrible way to die in your cell—even if that last bit about his dick was bullshit.

No one was charged with Lonnie's death. The news story said that a hair-brained inmate had botched a job on the TV set, and that Lonnie's death was due to the set being wired to the toilet, but that didn't make sense, if you asked me.

I didn't know what happened in his cell; I just knew it was a horrible way to die, especially after he made all that effort not be fried in the electric chair at the hands of the state.

What really got under my skin was how I heard about Lonnie's death.

Fucking Roland came back from the lieutenant's office one day, loudly calling out to me. He was crowing about my buddy, Lonnie, and how had been "cooked" in his cell, right downstairs from us. Roland shouted that Lonnie had just been "wheeled out dead on a gurney from out of the disciplinary cells below cooked to a crisp!" and yadda, yadda, yadda. I thought, *whatever . . . asshole!*

I waited for the investigating officers to come pull me out of my cell and speak to me about his death. I hated the Internal Investigations Division (or, as it was known, "I.I.D." It was the big brother of the kid who just split your lip open in the school yard. You were a suspect for anything done to *you,* is how it went with those people. That time, however, they never bothered me, and I was happy for it. I don't think they spent even ten minutes actually investigating Lonnie's death. It was such a funny story, because to them, Lonnie was nothing more than a joke.

One thing became clearer and clearer to me as the days went by in my cell with nothing to do, as I sat hearing all the guys around me having a blast listening to music, watching TV, or reading books. It was one thought:

Either Roland or I had to go.

Now, there was no other prison within Pennsylvania that was willing to accept me right then, so I figured I was going to have to make a move on him. What I didn't realize was that Roland was already, like, two chess moves ahead of me in our game. He was thinking the same thing I was—but *he* had help.

So Lonnie went to his grave, and I did "the walk of shame," with shit all over me. All I got out of it was some new paperwork, and having all my shit taken from my cell for, like, ninety days. Rump looked a lot smarter than me, right then, folks, he certainly did . . .

8

The Razor Dance Tango

I finished serving my disciplinary time in style for my part in Roland's snitch work. I bartered with Yahti for the use of a small AM radio set, and a half set of headphones. He charged me a fortune, and even made me buy new batteries, afterward, as well, for using his radio. But I liked him because he was such a little tight ass, who was always trying to hustle everyone, so I didn't complain about it to him. I was able to listen to the BBC's World Service, or a college football game, or even some music on my radio. So I did a little "easy time," once I had some new books sent over to me by some guys whom I had bartered with on the pod next to ours.

George even sent me over some of his food, in exchange for my citrus fruits and breakfast honey packets. He needed it because he was either making mead from the honey, or wine from the fruits. You could do your time "hard," or make your life behind bars passable as some did.

Once I was back to my routine with the other men, I skipped yard and day room altogether for weeks. I was dealing with all sorts of drama regarding my case, and my personal life on the outside was a mess.

The lawyers appointed to my case by the federal courts were about to do me dirty. I had finally gotten to the federal court level in the appeals process. It had *only* taken me ten years of appeals to get to that level of appellate courts in America, including eight years spent in the state appeals court, which was a complete waste of time. My escape from custody insured that my state court appeals didn't have a chance. Here was the issue:

I finally had to have my head "shrunk" by teams of psychiatrists, after all of those years of incarceration. It was done by a team of doctors hired by my own lawyers, no less.

Not only did I have to have my head "done in" by a team of "shrinks" that was bent on digging deep into that head of mine, but, no, sir, I *also* had to have the news delivered to me in the shittiest way possible.

The deal, I was told, was that since I had been raped at the age of seven, and my attacker had beaten my head in with a rock, all of that could be used to get me off of Death Row.

All of the previous lawyers assigned to my case knew, going in, that I never once requested any less of a sentence than what I had first been given: death.

I knew it would be a pathetic thing to do to me, but essentially my lawyers would say to the courts, "My client is innocent. My client is innocent. *But*, if that's not enough of an argument, let us tell you how his mind was broken by all that was done to him as a child."

They would plead with the court that although I was actually guilty, it was only because I was so pathetically broken mentally, and my life should be spared!

Fuck that, I thought. No way would I ever file anything like that with a court, where I begged anyone for my life, because, by doing that, I would then concede that I had no mind left.

Now I am not naming any of the lawyers who were representing me, simply because I loved those people who represented me on appeal. I know I could indulge myself in this book by pointing out who did all of that to me, but despite *what* they did, which gutted me personally, I am still grateful to them for my freedom today.

Sadly, though, as I have pointed out, I had to deal with a lot of issues during the time I was incarcerated, but each time I have tried to take the high road in speaking about those who tried to belittle me.

I had to work my ass off the most to be at peace with those times when lawyers either treated me like I was actually guilty and sold me out, or when they treated me like I was insane.

A second group of lawyers, at times, suggested that the organization, Innocence Projects, should use its resources elsewhere, because I was not right in the head, and that my effort to use DNA was a ploy.

A reporter from the *Delaware County Daily Times* newspaper told me that when he asked people from Innocent Projects about my case, he was told many times that my lawyers had told them (and other such groups) to pass me by because I was insane. I knew all of that even before I sat down with the federally appointed lawyers who were "taking my case in a new direction" with the doctors.

My visit with the lawyers about that issue went badly right from the start. The messenger who delivered the news was a guy who I really had no time for.

I got it, I told him. He was bright, and he was a good lawyer, and whatever else he might have thought, he was wrong. He was wrong to have made me go through a battery of psychiatric testing, just for the purpose of using the results in court, against my wishes.

What hurt was that he made me do that only to get the money needed to pay for DNA testing. I knew all along how he was thinking secretly that if the tests were inconclusive, he was going to ask the court to spare my life, because injury to my brain as a boy made me insane or diminished.

I was being fed a shit sandwich right then by my lawyers, and told to swallow it—and I knew it! It was all about how they had an "ultimatum" for me, too, which was: If I did NOT go through with the many hours of psychiatric testing they wanted me to endure, their office simply would not pay for any DNA testing while my case was in the federal courts.

As I sat in the visiting room talking to the lawyers, I bet that some guard behind me, who was hearing all about my dilemma over the phone system, was probably laughing his ass off. I fumed silently, not wanting to add to his glee.

They had me. The lawyers knew it. I knew it. And the guy on the phone in the visitation chair next to me with his hip-hop, dressed-up, white girlfriend (who had just popped her gum over the phone lines for the fiftieth time) knew it, too.

I had to sit there like a stooge while I was fed that crap by my lawyers, when all they had to do was call me from their offices over the phone lines.

I sat there with a stone cold heart, thinking maybe I ought to pull some real dramatic shit on them right then, thinking maybe I should just say "Fuck you!" But I knew that if I said that to them, I would dash any remaining hope that my mother and father had of me getting out, so I "bitched up," and tried another way.

In the end, I put up enough resistance to save face. I let it get to a point in the conversation where I let them have their way, all so I could get it over with. Because they never respected me for who I was, as a man, anyhow.

I made one statement to my lawyer, who was the main person in charge of deciding it all for me. I said the same thing to him that Yahti said to Busthead, the first time that Busthead looked at Yahti and told him that his butt looked "Yummy" and he wanted to eat it. My Boy, Yahti, had the whole day room laughing, when he yelled out, "Yeah, well you better make me *LIKE* it, motherfucker'!"

So, that day, with my lawyers basically grinding me up, I gritted my teeth hard, and listened their crap until I had enough.

With thoughts of silly ass Yahti saying what he had to Busthead, in order to keep myself from losing it, I simmered down. It appealed to me so much that I thought I would give it a go on my own lawyer.

I leaned towards the glass of the visiting room partition, and, holding the phone up close to my mouth, said, in a perfectly normal voice, "You better make me *like* this." Then, I hung up the phone and went back to my unit to handle all the other things on the floor that I had to hang onto — all while the doctors went to testing my head in the days to follow.

Right there is what got my head messed up about the unit. There was never a break from either the court battles, or the jailhouse battles; they just never ended. I was constantly under duress from some sicko in the pod, or the courts battles that constantly hung over me. If I wasn't having to deal with the guards or inmates, it was things going badly at home with my alcoholic brothers (or family) and their issues on the outside. My head was swiveling, just trying to keep it all under wraps, because of all of it.

With the time dragging by so slowly with the lawyers in court, and the courts not caring, or how I had poisoned my appeals with my escape, I was wearing down mentally. Added to all that was the new interaction with doctors, which was daunting.

I was so tired of it all that I went into a funk mentally, and began sleeping all day. I was being driven mad by all of the pressure, and I saw no end in sight anytime soon. I just "clicked off the lights" inside my head, and left the world for a few months, while they "shrunk" my head . . .

After a while, it felt as though there was something physically wrong, living like that. My body was reacting to all the sleep and lack of movement. I knew it was not the occasional "seasonal depression" that people could get from putting cardboard over the windows and not having any sunlight directly on them for years while living in a cell. No, I was *ill*.

Then, I became even more paranoid when Yahti suddenly died. How did a guy, at the young age of 21, who was standing there one day talking to me in the day room, just suddenly *die* overnight? No one had gotten to him physically, because his cell was locked. No one heard him hanging himself, and there were no cuts or marks on him that we could see, yet that kid never had a chance.

Yahti was not even 22 years old when he died. He had such a gregarious way about him that he was just plain fun to be living next to. I could not believe he was dead, just like that, wheeled right past me with the sheet up over his face on a hospital gurney . . .

It was Bobby who made it *his* show then. He and his racist ass wanted the event be remembered as funny afterward. He got on his door later that evening and called for George to get on his door, too. He lamely checked on his little winemaker friend, and asked how he was doing. Without waiting for a reply, he asked George if he had heard what killed Yahti. I knew some shit was about to be thrown out there for all of us to listen in on, so I got up on my door as well.

Upon seeing me at my door, Bobby smiled. He would surely lay it on thick, I thought. He asked George if he thought there was anything funny about the food being sent to Yahti by any of the other guys from the pod.

I said, "That's fucked up Bobby, don't *do* this," because I *knew* what he was going to do. Bobby *loved* to mind-fuck people. He was going to wind up George mentally about accepting any more food, but that was not the only issue. He was then also going to try to convince any of us listening that somehow *he* had slipped some poison into the food that he had given Yahti.

I groaned loudly at what he was doing, thinking, *Oh come one dude! Do you really need to give us all that crap right now?* I felt like saying it aloud out the door then, but I knew it was pointless.

So Bobby took George down "Bogeyman Lane" with his bogus tale of feeding poison to Yahti, and even he got George to sing along that he agreed, yep—and he did, indeed, remember that he'd seen Bobby give food to Yahti just before he died.

It was pathetic to hear him manipulate George into believing that he had seen any of that. But George said, "Yep, that's right, I recall it all, yes *sir*," and he complimented Bobby on his move to kill Yahti. Then, George said that, from then on, he was going to be especially careful to check the fruit that he had bartered with the black dudes for.

Yeah, right, I thought. That was like getting a four-year-old to remember, right in front of all of us, that he had gone to the Moon with his daddy.

I put my headphones over my ears, because it was just so lame to witness what was going on. Bobby could get all of them to wonder if he killed Yahti, but I could not have cared less.

I listened to my music to blot things out, because I knew all the while what he had done. If Yahti had died of natural causes, then so be it. But what if Bobby had somehow murdered him with poison? (Although I was certain that if he had, he'd have done it without anyone else being in on it.)

Yahti's death kind of messed with me for a while. I hated that fat fuck, Bobby, for laughing about it for weeks afterward, but I never tormented myself by believing in his bullshit. All I knew was that one day, I was standing there laughing and joking with Yahti, and the next day he was dead in his cell. When he died on the unit, it seemed like no one wanted to laugh, or joke about things much any longer. We couldn't even get Busthead to come over and entertain us with his antics during that time, and all my sympathy had to be put on hold.

You see, I had endured all of those psych tests my lawyers had me take, and anyone who had studied psychology for six years at a university level would have known how I felt. As a result, I knew what was coming in a report soon to be written by professionals.

I was eviscerated by having to tell strangers that I'd been raped as a boy, and that I'd been beaten in the head with a stone during the assault, which left me to deal with some "aphasia" [a loss of ability to understand or express speech]. (In spite of that brain damage, I can still do some remarkable things with my so-called diminished brain.)

They said I was damaged. I said so what? (I believe that regardless of once having brain trauma, that I can do remarkable things. One thing is obvious. I have talent as a writer, and my brain is lucid. Proof? I wrote this entire book that you now hold in your hands in only three days' time.)

There was no point in telling the doctors that my brain was as remarkable as it was back then, because I didn't want "grandiose megalomania" added to the final three psychological reports created by those who postulated that I was a crazy fuck, or who said I was suffering from all the bad things done to me as child. (I read those reports, and the words still sting.)

One thing I know for certain is that that experience left me with a sense of self assurance. No matter what they based their reports on, I was right and they were wrong all along. Anything else would just be me trying to rub their faces in it, so I won't bother.

And, of course, as was always the case with my truly messed up life, right after I finished all those nasty tests, I learned that all the biological evidence from my trial that had any value was now "gone."

That one made things really bleak for me . . .

As you might imagine, I should have been bitter as hell that I had been done like that — all so that my lawyers could get some psych reports to help them file a claim in court asking that I be given a life sentence.

I should have been bitter that all the evidence from my case had been lost, and that any DNA testing was pointless. I was surely stuck living in that hell hole. I should have been bitter for so many things right then, I guess.

I was going through some really bleak shit in that cell, dealing with the whole "Lonnie thing" being thrown at me inside the jail. I was so caught up with that, I was blind to anything else. And that nearly got me killed in the days following my exams. The only excuse I had for coming close to dying was that I was not on my game.

The incident occurred on a weekday, either a Monday, or Wednesday (I am no longer sure which one it was). I had so much shit going on in my head that I probably looked like a zombie to those around me during that time. I was awaiting my turn to come out of my cell and go into the shower, and was thinking how shitty everything was. I had a soap dish and wash cloth in one hand, and was wearing a towel over my boxer shorts. I sat on my bunk, lost in thought. I had a small bottle of shampoo in my other hand that I kept tapping on my thigh. I hated to wait.

When my door popped open remotely, I entered the shower area. I plucked the yellow plastic razor we were allowed to shave with from the metal bars on the shower room door, and went in and turned on the water taps. I took off my eye glasses and set them on the edge of the window in the shower.

At no time did I take note of which guard was on duty in the control booth, as I might have done if I'd had my shit together better. All I know is that, all of a sudden, with water running hard onto my head, I heard a door pop open on the pod. I was slow in turning my head, but when I did, I saw a brown blur of a human being in the doorway of the shower, and he was swinging at me. But he wasn't throwing punches, instead he had some sort of blade in his hand, and he was slashing at me with the thing! It was Roland!

I lunged at my attacker, and made contact with his head, hitting my head against his forehead with a real good *smack*. As I did that, he fell backward, and his feet slipped on the wet floor. My forward motion carried me with him, and I ended up falling to the floor alongside him, with both of us getting all tangled up in the eight-foot-wide, clear plastic shower curtain. I ended up on top of him, trying to grab him as he squirmed under me, but he had baby oil all over him (by design, of course), so I couldn't get a grip on his skin.

Roland got his hand free and slashed my face with his weapon, just over my right eye, narrowly missing my eyeball. Miraculously, I never lost my sight, even with all the blood running into my eyes from the cuts he made while slashing at me over and over. He cut my wrist deeply when I got his arm locked in mine. He tried to cut me with the blade locked between my hands. The only reason he failed was because of the plastic sheet of the shower curtain that was between my hand and his arm. Because of that, I was able to grip the blade long enough to pin my body against him. All the while he was wriggling hard to free himself, I was head butting him over and over.

We were both hyperventilating from being wrapped up in that plastic sheeting. Inside of a minute, we were both fighting for breath. I was getting so panicky that I was losing my mind, as that fucker tried his best to get that arm free and slash my throat. I nearly screeched in panic, because I was losing control of his arm.

Whoever was in the control room needed to push the panic button to send in the troops. All the guys on the pod were yelling so loudly for us to kill one another that the commotion was too big to ignore. Clearly it was not a "home crowd" for Roland, because most of those watching wanted me to kill him. Nearly everyone who was yelling from his cell was screaming at me to finish off that motherfucker.

I'm not bullshitting you, at the same time they began pulling us apart from the shower curtain, I passed out from the exertion.

Next thing I knew when I awoke was that I had new bandages all over my hands—and not a single personal possession was left in my new cell.

I had been tossed onto a pod without a day room at its center, right next to Gary, no less. Oh, and they took all my stuff *without* a disciplinary hearing, and nothing was allowed into the records on the pod about the incident.

Meanwhile, Roland had nothing done to him at all for the attack. He stayed in his same cell and kept all of his belongings. Of course, it was the guard who was a former cop, and who hated me, who was working in the control booth that day. It was he who had decided to let Roland out of his cell to get me—and *that's* why it was all hushed up.

I sat in my cell and thought it was now full-out war. I chuckled a little gallows chuckle, and hoped the power would go out, so Gary could go on stage and entertain me for a while.

I lay there with my new scars and lots of time to think about how I might get out—while I was still mentally undamaged. *And* I had to figure a way to get rid of anyone else who might try me next. Unless there were other power outages, my "old friend" Gary, next door to me, wouldn't get any chances to torment others. It was time for him to go, yes sir, and he brought it all on himself.

Gary demanded to be accepted as "sane" by the courts, and asked to be executed right after I was put on his pod. His story was a real news spectacle, especially because the so-called "epitome of evil" was now embraced by prosecutors as being indeed a sane man! They all said: "Good for you, Gary, for admitting you were just a criminal who was sexually depraved."

The usual battles played out in the Pennsylvania courts, and were shown in the media during the months leading up to his actual execution. Old Gary would be only the second man ever to be executed in Pennsylvania's recent history, and he knew he would be a star in the press for it all, one last time.

As he walked by my cell on his last day, he was heavily chained and was escorted by four of the biggest men I ever saw in guard uniforms. They were accompanied by an additional officer who was holding a camcorder on his shoulder, just like when Keith was executed. I looked right into Gary's eyes one last time, as he passed by me.

I have seen cold-hearted men with guns in their hands, on the verge of shooting someone, who looked like they did not have an ounce of remorse. Compared to Gary, they would have looked like nervous little children.

I have seen men so hate-filled that they emitted it like electricity from their bodies. Gary was somewhere between shitting himself—knowing they were finally putting him in "a pit," as he had done to others—and showing everyone with whom he made eye contact just how much he was *into* it all!

He had that "rock star performer" look about him, the kind where someone is so "lit up" in performance mode that they are all wild-eyed and excitable on stage. He had so much energy that he was bounce-stepping hard against the leg irons on his ankles—kind of like he wanted to get the show on the road, and he was *moving*!

It freaked me out to be that close to his energy. It was like being swept up in a crowd, and having the heavyweight champ slash through it.

When Gary reached me, I found myself taking a step backward inside of my cell, even though I was behind a steel door. It was as if I was trying *not* to catch a whiff of whatever mad poison it was he was drunk on.

A week after Gary passed by my cell, he was in the death chamber over in Rockview prison, right in the middle of the Pennsylvania Mountains, to where Keith had been moved. But the most gruesome events would play out all that week, and would culminate in one of the most pitiful pleas for mercy ever witnessed during an execution. No one could have imagined what happened and, to this day, I still have no idea why it was done.

One day, some nameless lawyer in some law office, came up with a brilliant idea to try and save Gary from the "dead man's call." He *or* she decided to create one *more* victim to be eaten alive by the saga. You see, without truly caring about the collateral damage it might cause, they simply chose to involve someone associated with Gary, whom they felt could sway the Governor of Pennsylvania from killing him. They went out and found his beautiful, young, bi-racial daughter.

Somehow, they got in touch with the child born of the rape and torture of the very first woman Gary had signed out of the mental hospital, way back in 1979—and actually convinced her to come forward and plead for Gary's life.

I watched the news broadcast of that little girl, who had been swept up in that shit, and who was not even twenty years old at the time, as she pleaded in the press for her "daddy" not to be killed. It broke my heart to see someone used like that, to hear her say that no matter how evil he was, or how mean he had been to her own mother, she wanted to love and forgive him.

It made me so sad, and I cried so hard, that I had to stop looking at TV all day after that. I was furious that those lawyers had used her like that. I'm sorry, but you just don't "go there" with some things like that.

When I think of the newspaper photos of that poor girl, surrounded by lawyers who personally did not care what they were doing to her, I feel like they were just as cold as Gary in trying to get what they wanted. I can only imagine what that girl was asked to do.

I can not understand what it must be like to plead for the life of the man who brought so much horror into your life. I admit I don't have that type of compassion inside me. And I don't think I believed in that kind of goodness *until* that day when she spoke. I was so proud of that little girl who showed us all, in her own words, that no matter what, we have no right to kill one another, that regardless of whether or not we have the "right" to do so, killing is *never* righteous.

The governor of Pennsylvania, at that time, was a right-wing Republican candidate, who thought he would be the next President of the United States. He had already put down one of my friends from Death Row when Keith went to his death in 1995, so I knew he would have no moral issue putting down Gary.

What happened next was well covered in the press and easy to fact check.

Gary was hell bent on making a last statement those final nine days before his execution. He was going to tell all of us his "glorification story," just as he had done in our cells when the power was lost. We would hear, one last time, all about his blessings from God to do all the things that he did to other humans.

They shaved him where they had to put intravenous needles into his flesh, then stuck him in a hospital gown, and put a catheter into his penis, as he lay there on a hospital gurney. They put a heart monitor on him, and then six officers wheeled him into the death chamber for the last stage of the execution.

I have no doubt that his heart was beating like crazy when they finally got him in there and inserted the needles into his arms, and especially when they hooked the needles inserted into his arms to the drug lines that would deliver the drugs to kill him.

I know there was a detailed and methodical routine to set him up like that for his farewell, and I'll bet you anything that he was as scared as a child of all that was being done to him. But, most of all, I'll wager any amount of money that Gary shit himself when they raised those curtains and he saw his daughter standing right there.

The way I heard it, they all said Gary completely lost it emotionally at the sight of his child. They said he was blubbering about how he wanted his baby girl to forgive him.

How pitiful he was during those last moments, when all that nasty, contrived bullshit left him, and he broke down over the love he felt for a child he had made during one of his sickest acts.

I felt for his child, as anyone surely would, but I just could not feel anything for him. He was so driven by his own madness that I didn't give a damn whether, all of a sudden, he felt some kind of love for a child whom he had produced during a rape and torture.

I just wanted his voice out of my head for good. I didn't want him to come back and be in the cell next to me any longer. Where they took him was of no concern to me either. I sat on the bed in my cell, on the top floor of Western State Penitentiary's Death Row unit and I said, "Fuck you, Gary, your whole act was bullshit anyway."

People wonder why I am not screwed up in the head after living around those kinds of people year after year. And, most of the time, I just don't feel like I have the energy to respond in detail. It was *so* crazy on so many levels that I had no choice but to be drawn into it all.

I must confess that back then (just as it does now), it fascinated me to know about that whole other world on Death Row. I mean it. The general public only sees the notorious killer being finally captured on TV, or reads about it in the newspapers.

People are able to watch gruesome stories on TV in a detached manner, while munching chips and drinking cold drinks, seated on their living room sofas. Me? I just ended up sharing my snacks or meals right alongside those twisted bastards for decades.

"That guy," who scares the shit out of you at night on TV, was standing in front of me, whenever I had to leave my cell. He was the guy I had to live with, and either befriend, or, alternatively, make sure that I never turned my back on. That was all very real for me.

As Gary was going through his weird death march, it all felt like a segue to what lay ahead for me next. I was losing hope, and my thoughts were becoming bleaker and bleaker. I even told my spiritual adviser to take away all of her bullshit, and to leave me to it for a while. I had no time to think about what would happen *after* I died, I told her, because there was too much shit going on before I ever got to that point.

9

"Get this shit off me!"

Ironically, I was in the shower, once again, over on my new pod, when the next incident occurred. A replacement-unit sergeant told me to get my white ass out of there right then, as he ran onto the block and checked to be sure there was an inmate inside each cell. It was nearly 2:00 p.m., and the daily 1:00 p.m. solo blast from the prison horn, which signaled that the general prison population head count was cleared, had yet to be set off.

Instead of the usual, single blast, what we all heard was the long, wailing noise of the riot horn that signaled an escaped prisoner. (If you go back and read the news accounts, you'll find that, at the time, what seemed like half a prison block had run away from the prison!)

Eventually, after a few hours, the staff of Pittsburgh Penitentiary learned that as many as nine men had tunneled out of the prison using power tools. They used drills and all manner of equipment that they had acquired with the help of some really lame industry workers.

Who were those people that were called "prison industry workers?"

But, first, let me tell you why local communities love prisons in the first place. You see, not just prison guards work inside a jail, there are hundreds and thousands of prison "industry/maintenance" workers who also enter a prison each day. Those folks are as powerful as the guards.

Back in Huntingdon, I learned that the guys who worked as supervisors in the kitchen warehouse coincidentally also owned a restaurant in town. It was easy to load up with free food from the state when the captain of security had his brother take truckloads of food from the jail (marked as "garbage") that then went straight into his restaurant kitchen.

Everyone had their hands out. The guy who ran the wood shop also had a side business doing furniture repairs. The guy who ran the farm on the prison grounds had a cheese business that sold all sorts of dairy products. The guy who ran the inmate commissary inside the jail double billed everything sent in so that his local store had free stock.

The system is a racket.

The one thing that put an end to those millions of dollars that were being stolen at Huntingdon for years was the accidental making of a sex tape by security officers. It was all undercover recording done by the security personnel who were watching the warehouse supervisor having sex with inmates who were working there. The inmates themselves were allowed to steal items from the warehouse in exchange for sexual favors.

The theft was so rampant at Huntingdon Prison, from where I had just come, that the Deputy Warden of Operations was bounced from his job for embezzling something like two hundred thousand dollars of funds from the prison.

The average American does not realize that there are a hundred ways to rip off the state through its prisons, and how it is done all the time, and so easily that it's really a joke.

The point of all of this is that I found it incredible that not one person from the "prison industry" was fired for allowing nine men to escape. Oh, sure, a couple of guard administrators were shuffled around to other prisons, but the industry workers all kept their jobs. That's power.

I saw the Governor of Pennsylvania land in his helicopter right by my window, on the big parking area below me, after the escape.

He came there to have a look at the forty foot tunnel that no one had noticed being dug for months and months, with the press in tow, to show how angry he was.

But heads hardly rolled over the big event. Instead, we were just on lock-down for a long while, because every single cell inside of Pittsburgh Penitentiary then had to be searched.

It was two solid weeks of no yard, no day room, and no phone calls home. I just went to sleep and waited for at least half of my belongings to be tossed away (as always happened during searches, every time someone escaped, or we had a riot to clean up after). When things happen somewhere in a jail as large as ours, they trim the fat from the whole prison with a massive search. Once they take everything they can from you, they chuck it all into giant carts, and it's tossed away.

It was actually those men who had escaped from the general population who became the link to my getting out of that place in a way that was so weird I could not have made it up.

Of course, it all came down to the one guard who had been tormenting me the whole time. He had finally become bored with his usual efforts to make each day really dark for me. How did he do it? *Why* did he do it? It was Roland who finally got me set up right.

It started with my food. You are fed twice on the day shift, and then you are fed once more on the evening shift. Breakfast usually is at 7:00 a.m., and then you have lunch at about 11:30 a.m. If the guard who feeds you on the evening shift hates you, he spits in your meal, or clears his nostrils into your food once a day. And, if it's the guard on the day shift who does it to you, you have lost *both* early meals each day.

I did not have to do much to earn the title of "My Favorite Rapist-Murderer" from my chief tormentor, "Double D." I counted the men there who had convictions similar to my own. At the same time "Double D" was spending feverish amounts of time tormenting me alone, I was living on a unit that had at least a dozen or more rapist-murders (some of them were even multiple offenders). So, it was not a rare offense by any means. I was not singled out for my *crime*; I was singled out because of the dirtiest of lies.

Roland was so good at conning the guards that he managed to spend lots of time hanging out with them in the sergeant's office. He would be in there chatting with them about whatever prison shenanigans he claimed to have knowledge. He used that opportunity to snag a photo from a work folder that belonged to "Double D." It was a photo of that guard's grandchild taken at a playground. At first, I bet Roland took it to use for his own sexual self abuse, because that was his thing to do. But then he got his boyfriend, Marty, involved somehow, and together they got poor George to be the "set up" guy for their little ploy.

Roland convinced Marty to get to George in the law library and tell him that if he sent me a note asking for "that young stuff," it would mean that George wanted me to send over some fresh fruit to him from my pod. Sure as shit, George did as he was asked, and wrote a note and gave it to Marty. They never passed me anything, but now they had George willing to say he wrote a note if needed.

Then, during the meeting that Marty had with George in the law library, he typed a note that they claimed was from me to George in reply. They said the note came with the photo that was sealed up in a bag. I saw that note in the "Double D's" hand later on at my cell, when he waived it around and yelled in my face.

I had Sgt. Rage and "Double D" my door that day and it was as ugly as it could get. They got control to open my door, and then stood in my doorway like they wanted to bash my brains in. Both men were furious at me, and stood in my face and demanded answers about what they claimed I had done. The stench of booze from the previous night's drinking seeped from Sgt. Rage's pores, making me blanch in disgust at the smell.

He stood inches from my face, his spittle flying everywhere as he said what a sick fuck I was. He said menacingly, "If you fuckin' *blink*, I will club your head in right now!" Then he steadied himself and asked me, "Now, did you lift this officer's photograph of his granddaughter out of his folder?"

The blood drained from my face when I saw my note to George in his hands, along with the image. I looked as guilty as fuck, despite myself, and he took my recognizing that note as admission that I had done it. He bit his lip in fury and made a low sound as he seethed with angry thoughts. He just slid my door closed and said, "'Oh, you dirty motherfucker, you are gonna *wish* I had just beaten your rotten brains out."

I never said anything in response. What was the fucking point?!

Each morning after that event, "Double D" began greeting me loudly in the same routine on the pod. It was *always* the same:

"Gooooooood morning to my favorite Rapist-Murder!" followed by "And how are *you* this fine day, you sicko?" Then it would be the splatter of snot expelled from his nostrils into my food, or a mouthful of spit from that nasty morning-breath mouth that he would splatter into the tray of food.

Then, with a flourish, he would slam the pie hole shut as hard as he could to make sure he sent my food tray flying into my cell. (No coffee for me, thank you.) He usually followed that up with maniacal laughter after he had shoved the now-destroyed food fully into my cell. Each time, I stood very still, and well away from my door, while waiting for him to do what he did to me. Then, I recited the same thing by rote every single time: "Thank you, Officer."

There was no way that I was going to last there then, since it had been going on twice *every* single day for nearly a full year. And that's no bullshit, either. Each day, the same thing, over and over, followed by my words, "Thank you, Officer ."

At first, I figured that I would endure that shit for maybe a few weeks, a couple of months at most, surely, but that sick shit went down all day, every day of that last, agonizing year I was there.

What I finally had to do to get out of that place without being killed, or killing someone, was quite sad. I would have to let that creature of a guard hurt me so badly that they would have to get me out of there. I also had to come up with a way to get someone involved, who was big enough within the prison system, to back me up, and to make sure that they got me out of the unit before it was too late.

Meanwhile, I was so angry at having my food toyed with twice a day that, at times, I thought about how I could cut it all short. I could just throw up my hands, and say, "Fuck it all." I could let all of his tormenting drive me to just kill "Double D" right then and there.

I mean, I could have done it to him without ever having left my cell, in light of all of the weapon-making knowledge that I had. All I needed was a pair of undershorts and a magazine to kill him—*if* I really wanted him dead.

When you are being openly tortured, it is so hard to not think of some dark things. I had days when I had nothing left to hope for, compounded by the presence of a whole gang of folks around me who wanted to see me suffer as much as humanly possible. It all made me bite hard on that poison apple called bitterness. At times, I wanted others to feel the same shit that they were doing to me. I hated how my mind was shaped during that time to lose caring or feeling for anyone. My mind was filled with poison, as I thought of the different ways men killed in prison.

I did not originate those styles of combat weapons. I learned my shit from others who used those weapons on me mostly. I just thought of ways to refine them as best I could, if the need arose.

There are three basic types of "remote killing tools" to lash out with that you can make while inside your cell. This is how I learned how to make each one:

The first one was nasty to learn.

I was in the Delaware County jail, early on in my prison time, when I learned how to make a "SNAG." I was under serious duress from physical attacks in my first few weeks of incarceration.

Being accused of a sex-based, abduction and murder case at the age of twenty meant that I would be challenged or tormented by anyone inside who saw me as being weak. A local motorcycle gang, whose members were locked up with me on my cell block, made it even worse. It had five members on my cell block who toyed with me daily because they thought I was an informant.

With them on my back each day, making my life miserable, the rest of the broken bastards who were also there soon felt free to do all sorts of dirty things to me as well.

On D-Block of the old Delaware County prison where I was housed, there were two, long tiers of cells, twenty-four cells in length (there was a bricked-off area of another twelve cells), with a two-way, swinging door built into the adjoining walls at the rear, to gain access back there.

This extra rear area was all created for the section where the child molesters were housed. It was called J-Block. Once you went in there, you were never allowed around other men again.

With two cells used as shower rooms, that meant there were ninety-six men locked up on that block in the Delaware County jail. Within those ninety-six prison cells were those men who were charged with murder or other serious crimes only. Mixed in with that basic group of men, oddly enough, were also those men who had been put there for disciplinary punishment within the prison.

So, basically, D-Block in the Delaware County prison was as nasty as the state penitentiary. When you house men in separate cells for punishment reasons, who have nothing in their cells, and mix them in with the men who have been put there only awaiting trial, it always leads to bitter resentment. The ones who have it easy always abuse the ones with nothing.

Me? I had nothing, and I was one of the downcast. I was treated with resentment or scorn by ninety-nine percent of the guys there, during the first days of my being charged.

I was so young that most either wanted to fuck me, or they wanted to just kill me (especially the angry ones). Overall, they really just wanted to make me so miserable that I would kill myself. In fact, because of all the abuse and torture I had to face alone those first few weeks, I tried to hang myself. Being cut down by a guard, and being told that I was not allowed to "cheat the state" out of my punishment was very humiliating for me.

That was followed by a week spent chained by all four limbs to a hospital bed, and being left out in a hallway in my own filth because they made me shit or piss without a bed pan to use.

After I tried to hang myself that first year, I decided to fight it out. No matter what was done to me, I saw that I *had* to go on — especially after my mom cried in the prison hospital ward at my bedside, while inmates who went past us to get their medication, with an officer, "cat called" at her. Some guys made "crybaby" motions, with the backs of their hands curled over each eye in mocking fashion of a child crying at me, as my mother turned in embarrassment from their taunts. What a shit moment.

Sometimes in jail, I was injured when I was not always able to see attacks coming, like when a guy just jumped out of a cell, holding a weapon, and we went at it in hand-to-hand combat.

I could try to put my mattress up inside of my cell, but a guy put a blade on the end of a broom handle and tried to put my eye out with it (it hurt like hell when I got jabbed). I might be able to duck or close my eyes when someone tossed a mixture of piss and borax cleanser at my eyes, as I had to do a few times in the past.

What I hated most was how you could be gotten at by others in such sick ways, by methods that you had no defense from—even if you were looking.

At that point, because of the ongoing abuse targeting me, I was made to come out of my cell, all by myself, to exercise for two hours on the block interior. This was done after all the others had their exercise time in unison during the day. The captain of the guards said that I was not to be out of my cell when any other guy was out of his cell.

This "SNAG" effort was set up so cleanly that it should have actually succeeded in getting me killed. It happened when I was called out by another inmate near the back of the top tier located on D-Block. He said he had a newspaper that he wanted me to take from his cell to another man's cell while I was out exercising on the block.

Anyway, I went to fetch the newspaper, and I was midway down the tier (with the guy actually waiving the paper in his hand, like I should hurry and keep my focus on him), when I was distracted. Another guy, in a cell I had just passed, waited a beat, then tried to get me to look at what he said he had sticking out of *his* cell saying, "Nick, look here, I need you to get *this,* too . . . "

As I turned to look back over my left shoulder at the new voice calling me, I never saw the "SNAG" being lowered over my head . . .

I still get chills each time I think of how I felt when the smooth newspaper (rolled into a ten-foot-long pole) was slid across the back of my neck. I can still feel the cutting pain on my throat from the bed sheet material attached to it that had been made into a braided noose, which was burning hot when it was yanked on hard. When my head was slammed into the cell bars of a guy's door, it felt as though it had been yanked off, and I was shocked into fighting back. Terror shot through me, as I grasped at the noose on my neck. There was only one thing that made a difference—*really.* I wore corrective eyeglasses.

The guy's name was Curry—David, Donald, Darrell. I can't recall anymore, and don't give a shit *what* his name was. He was a fat, nasty, big old black dude from the city of Chester, Pennsylvania. He was doing life for the ugly murder of some girl whom he had abducted, raped, and then murdered in the seventies. He was easily two hundred and eighty pounds, dark complexioned—and fat. His hair was styled in a medium length "fro" haircut left over from the seventies. You could tell that this hair had once been pressed and straightened flat.

All four of his front teeth were missing, but the rest of his remaining teeth were huge, so he looked like a giant, angry sloth when he talked.

Curry made the snag he had hooked around my neck by taking newspaper and rolling it tightly, while feeding in more sheets of paper, until he managed to make a ten-foot-long pole. Now, the pole did not have to be strong, it only had to be sturdy enough to hold out a length of bed sheet that has been corded into a rope. The sheet had been made into an inch-wide line, with a big noose fashioned onto the end, which was about three feet in diameter. There was a "T" made from a second bit of newspaper tied to the end of the pole, so that the noose stayed open. Imagine a dog catcher's noose on a rickety, handmade pole . . .

All you had to do then was to find a way to get someone like me to walk down the tier, pass your cell, and then trick me by getting someone else to get me to turn my head long enough for you to stick the pole out of *your cell bars and over my head* (while it was held high enough to be above my line of sight, of course). Once it was over my head, you would simply drop it around my neck and pull.

When they did this shit to me, I reacted as fast as I could. The newspaper was angled poorly, so that it was across my head, because I flinched. Curry yanked on the pole and rope, and snagged me with the noose across my face. The rope, a ribbon of sheet material that had been soaked in water to make sure it did not break, was cutting me deeply. My eyeglasses got caught between the noose and my flesh on the right side of my face, just across my cheekbone. Lucky me.

The eyeglass frame was driven into my face so hard that the lenses popped out, leaving just the plastic frame there. I got two fingers into the gap on my face and twisted my neck at the same time. I managed to get the noose under my chin, and then I turned forward and around. The noose was on the back of my neck then, and my head was being pulling downward. The pain was excruciating, and Curry had slammed his body down on the floor of his cell, while trying to bash my head on the bars over and over, as I fought him.

I used my knees to brace myself against his efforts against the door of his cell, and both knee caps felt as though they would break. He was down on the floor, with his feet braced against the inside of the door frame, and he was yanking hard. My fingers were breaking, and today I have twisted-up fingers, or broken joints in my hands, from him putting so much pressure on my hands that my fingers snapped, one by one.

About thirty seconds into the attack, the guard came down the tier, just as my strength was waning. I was doing all that I could to deal with the horrible pain in my hands, face, and neck. The guard told Curry to stop. *Yeah, right.* And, of course, while all of that was going on, the inmates were yelling at a fevered pitch for the guy to finish me off.

The guard nervously took out a pen knife from his pocket and started sawing on the rope to free me. When he did that, everyone went berserk, yelling because it felt as though the ending was a dud. They were telling Curry to snap my head off if he could. When the rope was finally cut free, my head hit the railing of the tier behind me as I fell backward. Then, everything in my vision went white . . .

So, that is how you made a weapon to try to kill someone while they were outside your cell, and you couldn't get your hands on them. I had no hope of doing any of that on my pod. I wouldn't waste my time doing such gruesome thing anyway, *especially* after having it done to me.

And that brings me to the next attempt on my life. We'll call it "juice them!"

You really have to be lucky and clever to electrocute someone in jail. There are actually two ways to use electricity to kill someone in prison — or, at least to try.

The first way is obvious. You get a bunch of salt packets that come with your meal, or save up all the salt available. Then, you strip off the plastic coating on the wire on the electric cord of a TV set. You then take the cord and attach the two bare wires to your cell bars.

You flood the cell floor with water, then sprinkle the salt all over the wires, while you plug the TV cord into an outlet. If you do it at the very moment that a guard touches your door, you might be able to get him. This method is pretty lame, and is hardly ever lethal. Circuit breakers will pop, shutting off the power most times.

No, the best use of electricity as a murder weapon is "The Blaster." (Thankfully, I did *not* learn about this method by having it demonstrated on *me*.) I actually learned about it when I escaped from prison.

I was lucky enough (or unlucky enough) to land in a very famous prison in the state of Florida called "The East Unit," which is actually Starke Penitentiary, located in Northern Florida. That is where they put me when I handed myself over to authorities, after my escape in 1985.

I was in that prison for the hottest six months I ever spent in jail, all while locked inside of a cell located over a swamp. I was only there until I was to be sent back to Pennsylvania, and I was *not* to be executed like my neighbor there, the infamous Ted Bundy (talk about someone who was both a monster *as well as* a madman!).

I was in the only prison at that time in the state of Florida that did not allow anyone to possess any type of matches *or* cigarettes while within its walls. Cigarettes and matches of any sort were banned because they were the key ingredients in making a "blaster." Here is how to that weapon was made:

Men in that Florida prison took a two-foot piece of hollow pipe from their beds. They then crimped one end of it and sealed it with plastic melted from toothbrushes. They wrapped it even tighter with bed sheet material at that end. The crimped, molded end became a handle, or the base of a shotgun. They got a nail, or screw, and made a hole in the side of the pipe about an inch above the handle, which was big enough for one wire of an electrical cord to fit into. That would then be sealed with melted plastic so that no metal was touching wire. The bare wire was packed inside of the charge which was inside the pipe. The cord wire (which would also be bare) was then set against the outside of the pipe to make contact as well.

Then, an endless amount of matches and striker bits would be used to fill the pipe. They would be crushed up and mixed with the striker strips made of flint. (Carefully scraping off flint material from the match books with a piece of metal is very crucial to creating an explosion.) All of the ingredients would then be mixed together with kitchen salt, pebbles, and shards of glass. That mixture would then be tightly packed into the metal tube until there was enough inside to set off a good charge.

All you had to do then was stand at the door or window of your cell, and wait for a guard or inmate that you wanted dead to walk past. At the moment the victim passed the cell, the guy holding the "Electric Shotgun" would aim it at the victim's head while simultaneously plugging the electrical cord into the wall socket inside of his cell. Then the blast would blow your brains out all over the cell block tier. (I have personally seen actual "pock marks" all over the cell block walls inside the East

Unit from guys who were blasted there.) "The Blaster" is a bad-ass weapon.

Those were some "next level shit" methods, and I was really glad that I was under so much security in that Florida jail, where I was literally placed above the electric chair. On Q-Wing, where they had our cells "within cells," I was safe from all that. Yep. I was actually in a cell within a set of bars that had a big solid door to shut me in.

It was bleak, alright, but I was safe, as well, I learned, from shotguns in the wing of that one jail.

So that brings me to the last way of getting to someone whom you cannot get to physically while you are locked inside of a maximum security cell. And, all you really need are a pair of underwear, a magazine, and good ol' tobacco.

Tobacco is *so* precious in jail that it's nearly impossible to actually put a value on it in the normal sense. You see, if you mix urine and feces with tobacco in a cardboard milk carton, you can actually boil it into a poison.

All you do is fill the carton with those ingredients, then pierce two holes through the container near the top. You then thread a string through those holes, and it serves as a "handle." You hold the carton by its string handle, and cook the poison over heat. The more tobacco, the stronger the poison.

Next, you take toilet tissue and make paper "donuts" that are set afire while resting on the lip of the toilet bowl.

To make the "donuts," you first roll the toilet paper around your flattened hand until you have about a half-inch-thick wrap. You pull the paper off your hand and carefully fold the ends, making "pants cuffs," which are folded inward at each end. That is very important, because the paper will not give off any smoke at all as long as you fold the paper inward.

Once you have the "donut" lit, hold the milk carton over the flame and boil the poison. A good concoction takes days to ferment. If you keep adding more tobacco each time you boil the thing (about half a dozen times), you should come away with a "tar-based" poison.

Then you have to make a delivery system.

You take the underwear they make you wear on Death Row and carefully un-thread the waist band material from the underpants. You must be careful not to damage the elastic part, because that is the material you'll need to braid into an even stronger braid. That rubber material, when braided, is so strong that it will propel an object up to twenty feet with enough power to go through a simple wooden door.

Then take a perfume card from a magazine advertisement and pop both staples out of the magazine's spine. Turn those into a cone shaped dart, reinforced by wrapping the thread from the underwear around the staples. Make sure it has lots of loose threads to soak up the poison, with the metal tips of the staples entwined to a point at the tip.

Take more material from the underwear and bind the braided elastic band that you've made onto the base of the rolled up magazine. You want the dart to be able to go through the tube you created without much friction.

Once you've made the tube, practice pulling the elastic cord back about five inches (without the dart coming out), to where you can aim it level before letting go of the rubber band that propels the dart.

When your target comes into view, you aim for the neck, trying to pierce the main jugular vein. Your hope is to simply get enough poison into the victim, and do enough damage to his neck that he will die from the combination of both the injury and the poison. (It is a horrible thing to do to some guard, while he is handing you a bit of mail at your cell window.)

A prison guard doesn't stand a chance when his neck is only inches from your weapon and you drive that dart nearly out the back of his throat on impact, which sends him choking and gasping onto the floor.

That's why it takes a lot of guts to walk past a cell as a prison officer. You can't help but be on your toes all day, especially knowing that all this stuff is real.

Now I'll describe some of the "cheapo versions" of the last weapon system I described, using a minimum of items.

I once saw guys use a metal spoon to shoot an officer in the eyeball. I also saw someone else take a metal ink pen and shoot it into some inmate's neck (it went clear through), killing him. This weapon system is the most dangerous to deal with, because there really isn't much a person can do about it when it is sprung on them.

What a God awful sound it is to hear a man scream as he is shot in the face with a catapulted spear or dart. The only thing worse is being jabbed with a four-foot-long fluorescent glass tube that has been broken off and reinforced with wet sheets. I saw one of them jabbed into an officer's eye on my block in Huntingdon prison, back in 1989. His eye came out, and they kept jamming the tube into his face, over and over, anyway.

Every day, the guard who tormented me most goaded me by reading my mail over the intercom, in addition to spitting or "snotting" into my food. Of course, he also made sure that I lost my exercise or day room time as much as he could. In addition, he told the other officers on the unit that I was "X'd." That meant he had put crosshairs on my back, and they were all to fuck with me as much as possible to please him.

When Roland failed to kill me, that guard knew he was stuck there with me. What he hated most was my looking at him, and my knowing what I knew about him, because then he couldn't put on his "I am an okay guy" act with other inmates in front of me. So, as far as he was concerned, I either had to be terminated, or made so miserable that I would kill myself.

I had all that shit aimed at me day and night, while my spiritual adviser, in her letters to me, pleaded for me to not do anything completely "UN-fixable" (talk about asking a lot of me).

I tormented myself for being such a chump, and being played by my lawyers to have my head "shrunk." I agonized over having all of the biological evidence from my case deliberately trashed. The way my appeals were being handled by people who didn't care about what it did to me mentally robbed me of hope.

On and on it went, crushing me, and then, in 1998, when it seemed things couldn't get worse, my wife, Jacqueline, left me. (I hadn't written about her until now, because this was supposed to be about the unit. I felt all along that the one thing that I could do for her was to shield her from all of the things I had dealt with inside.

Jacque would see my broken bones, or she would see new scars on my face and body, but I never let on just how bad it was back then. I could not bear to think of the mental anguish that she would have had to live with if I described how poor George was abused sexually over a phone call during a visit with her. Why do that shit to your loved ones?

Until now, I have spared you from reading about my wife. I haven't described the added sorrow of being in love with a woman for nine years, a woman I actually married during a Death Row ceremony in 1988, believing at the time that I would go free when the DNA tests proved me innocent.

Her belief in me, while I was suffered, was a big reason why I was able to keep fighting. I've kept all of that sorrow out of this book, because no one needs to really know all that transpired in my marriage while I was going through the bleakest of times in that hell hole.

There's nothing I can add that could describe how she chose the worst possible time to leave me — especially THEN.

I swear, I've held back a lot so it wouldn't seem like I was overly stating how miserable the three-year ordeal of the appeals process had made me. The only point of my telling you all of this now, is because while that man tormented me on the unit every day, once Jacque left me, and he taunted me over losing her, there was really no good personal reason left for me not to kill him.

When my wife walked out of my life, I did an amazing thing. In fact, I have told the story many times over.

You see, I tell everyone that I wrote Jacque a really beautiful letter when she left me. I describe how, in the letter to my departing wife, I told her how much she meant to me, and how she had taught me to become a better man by loving me. I've gone into great detail about that moment when I've been filmed, and in the memories I share with friends when telling stories of my time with Jacque.

What I *never* tell people, and what truly mattered, is what I have already told you: that those bastards read all of our mail. I told you that no communications left the unit or came in without them sniffing through them like a dog seeking treats. So, yes, the guard who tormented me most took great pleasure from that most emotional moment in my life.

This sadistically driven man, who should never have been allowed to be a prison guard in the first place, sat in the control booth one day and turned on my intercom as a joke. He thought he was really funny, as he began to read my "letter of goodbye" to Jacqueline. On top of it all, he did so in the most condescending manner he possibly could.

That pathetic, broken man of a guard laid it on thick at times, especially when he got to my words about our marriage ending. He did so, as he chuckled about my wishing her and her "new" man all the happiness that they could find together. My heart was in my throat, as I leaned against the wall and pressed the button on the intercom, pleading with him to just mail the letter out. I did not yell or scream, I just begged him to please have mercy, and that I was sorry for whatever he thought that I had done to deserve all of that. I begged and I begged, long after he had clicked off the switch to the intercom, leaving me standing there, begging the wall . . .

Do you see what I mean? That shit just made me want to get it all over with. I had seen Keith check out of there only five months in that stinking pile of twisted humanity. I was already into my third year of that shit, and I was starting to crack. I couldn't take it much more, and I knew it. I was 450 miles from any family, I no longer had any connection to reality there with my folks, and the possibilities for my appeals, or hopes in court, were so bleak that I knew things were coming to an end.

Of course, with my life being the way it had always been, you would know that in order to have such a simple request as an exit from that place granted to me, it just *had* to be complex and twisted!

Thank God that I am nearing the point where I can move on with my life; that is how I feel after writing this all down for you, the readers. For years, I felt I'd never be able to tell anyone about the huge sidetrack my life took into the ultra insane world of my story. This was the hardest book I ever wrote, and yet, writing it was also the best thing I could have ever done at this point in my life.

So let's do this: metaphorically, let's get the fuck out of Pittsburgh Penitentiary, because I hope to God that I never have to go back to such a dark place again. Although the next chapter is the last, it's worth reading to learn how it all played out, and how I finally got out of jail once and for all.

But first, one last thing.

Every day I recited a mantra—a series of words that I said aloud as soon as I could stand upright, before my locked cell door. It wasn't anything flowery, or something I stole from someone a lot smarter than I was. I simply stood there every day and said to myself:

"I gotta get the *fuck* out of here!"

And those were exactly the last words I said to myself the day that I had my hand shattered in a metal cell door by the officer on my pod, who had been tormenting me for three years.

That was all it took to get out of that place—eleven broken bones in my left hand, which would be mangled for the rest of my life. Believe it or not, all I am saying is that I am *grateful* that I *only* had to give away full use of one of my hands for the rest of my life in order to get out of jail.

10

Kill, or Keep Your Vows

I miss some things about being in the prison system. I miss the way life was so precious at times, that the smallest of things were held aloft as gifts from the gods.

I read a series of books once; they were about a man named "33 Rabbit." He was a Toltec King from eons ago in time. He was so in love with his favorite drink made from cocoa that he declared a law stating that, if anyone but his royal family drank or ate it, they were to be beheaded as punishment. Then, their heads would be hung on sticks afterward to make sure that everyone knew why the king said no person could have that treat except him.

I remember that when I finished that book about "33 Rabbit," I went over to the paper sacks in my cell that held my commissary items, and I got out a chocolate bar and unwrapped it. I stood by the window and ate it, as I told Keith, through the vents, that I was thumbing my nose at "33 Rabbit." He asked me what the hell kind of pills I was taking. I told him the story about the Toltec people.

I told Keith the same thing rang true about power: The ones stopping others with their power are always the ones taking from everyone else.

Keith liked the way I described the work written about those people, so I passed the books over to him. He read all four books in the series in *two days*. He was a demon when you gave him new material to absorb. We shared lots of books in that same passionate way, mostly so that we would have something to talk about.

I loved talking to Keith. We had some of the most brilliant conversations about the things we read. We talked about how I had a wonderful plan for my death when it was time for me to go, based on the many books I had read during all the years I spent locked up in solitary confinement.

Some might say that I should have kept my stupid mouth shut about what I did with Keith right before the days when he asked to die. I see now that what I did was the "worst thing" that I could have done to someone else at that moment. I still have a hard time when I think about it, even today.

I beat my stupid-ass up over what I did for many days after it happened, and I hate how clever I was forced to be through it all. Yeah, but there's one thing I learned from that experience: No good deed goes unpunished.

On the night before he asked to be put to death, I spoke to Keith through the vents, and I mostly told him about what I had in mind for my own death. I told him how I'd come to the reasoning about the event, and that I was going to face my death with dignity. I said that he should end his life there, while he still could, by doing the same thing. I explained it as best I could, including the reasoning behind my decision.

Here is how I saw it all: *I* was the only one who could kill Nick Yarris. I know that is not a normal thing to say, but it was actually true of both who I was as Nick Yarris, the entity, and who, in fact, could kill him as he existed. My way to die, of course, was to be executed by the state. But I was going to do so on my terms, after I showed them how I had already killed off the person they thought me to be.

I told Keith that the many thousands of books that I had read in my life were now the tools that I was using to take my life. I told him that, unlike his life before prison, mine was spent fucked up as a junkie before I got arrested. He was never into drugs, or shit like that, so I had to explain further.

I explained how it all came to me when I was twenty-four years old. I had just been returned to prison after my escape in Pennsylvania. I told him that, right then and there, I knew I had made such a mess of things that my old life was essentially dead after my escape — and that since my life, the one as Nick Yarris, was over, I had only one mission from that point forward.

I was going to work to erase the foul-mouthed, poor-speaking, and ignorant person that I once was. I was going to replace him with a man I loved and respected. I explained that the only way to get through being executed was for me to erase everything that *they* thought

I was up until that time. I would prove that the broken human being I was once was long gone, well before they killed me. He asked me how I meant to pull that off.

I told Keith that I knew when I was being executed, I would not have the ability to hold a piece of paper and read from it aloud. I told him that I had worked so hard for so many years, practicing in my cell how to speak beautifully for just one reason. I did so, hoping that when I was in the death chamber, I would have what I wanted to say committed to memory, and would have the balls to say it all perfectly.

Keith asked me if I could recite my prepared speech to him all at once, as I would at the moment when I had to do so. I tried. It was hard, man. It was *so* hard emotionally to do that in front of him.

I felt my throat constrict with emotion, as he listened to me appreciatively. Before I spoke, I pictured him trying conjure up in his mind the image of them taking my life, all while he was conjuring up the scenario of his own death march.

I began my speech for Keith. It went like this:

"I am nothing to you. I know that just like the neutrino that emanates from the Sun and passes right through this earth, that I am going to pass from your life without much more notice than that of a neutrino.

"Whatever you think that I am does not matter any more. I have found a way to love myself and respect who I am. I am able to forgive you for taking my life because I wasted it with stupid acts of a child. I gave it away long

before you found me and it does not matter anymore how I die. I have been able to finally love myself.

"I have tried very hard to learn all that I was able to about this life so that before you took mine from me, that I could love everything about it.

"I am sorry that I did not find this all out sooner, and I hope that my family will remember how hard I tried to show them love."

That was it.

Keith said that it was really very well done, even if it was not his way of seeing things.

When I was giving my speech to Keith, I flubbed a part, but I nearly did it as well as I do in the dreams that still come to me now, even though I am free from those days.

Keith said that *he* would not have any big words for them. That was when I knew I had fucked up. I knew right then that I was confirming for him that he was doing the right thing. But then, I swear to God, I also thought about how he wasn't any more more capable of defending himself than George had been. It really affected him to see what Bobby had done with his dick to that poor guy in the day room. I knew he was too frigging meek to handle the mental brutality of a sexual assault.

I could have pulled back then, but I was not really able to just step away from the feelings of describing my own demise to the man. Otherwise I couldn't have gotten out the Bible and shared my feelings about being executed with Keith. I read the following passage to him, as a way of bringing a sense of meaning to him:

> "Let every person be subject to the governing authorities. For there is no authority except from God, and those that exist have been instituted by God. Therefore whoever resists the authorities resists what God has appointed, and those who resist will incur judgment."

Then, I told Keith that he had been lawfully judged by man in court, and now he had been lawfully sentenced by man to die. If he fought his sentence in that light, he was actually disrespecting God. I explained that both he and I were not actually able to pay back society for what we had done; we could only pay spiritually for our actions in life by how we died.

Then, Keith got real quiet on me, and I asked only what he thought this was doing to his folks. I asked him how long he wanted this to go on for them. He never answered me. Instead, he said we needed to wrap things up, and I knew what he meant by that. I told him that I loved him, and that he shouldn't be a dickhead and think too much about the things that I had just told him.

He told me that he was going to sleep. And that was the last of my friend, forever.

I guess I sent him to his death the best that I could. I did so, rather than to see him suffer on and on, under conditions that he had no chance against. He lived daily with pain beyond measure, and he was sorrowful. That man paid enough for all that he did on the outside. I don't feel the same way that you, the reader, might about this, probably because I lived next to him. I only beat myself up about it because of things that were not really part of his actual dying. I have to live with the thought that he might have made it to another prison, somehow, or if he could have gotten his sentence reduced.

I heard this Italian saying once. It went: "There is no justice without life."

My friend there without *any* hope for justice. I made sure that he got what little hope he could, as he listened to me, while he finished with his appeals. I know exactly how he felt when he went to his death. I know exactly how he felt, as well, when he wrote to the courts and asked to be put to death. I promise you that I know every single thing he faced when he asked to die like that.

I know all of that because I asked to die exactly as I had taught him how to do it.

I told Keith the truth: He had the power to stop all of this suffering by giving his life back to God. He could end it all by demanding that his lawful sentence be carried out. I told him that if he was able to love the person that he was right then, he should care enough about that person to end his misery. He should do so before who he was as a human being was erased.

I did not get my wish like Keith did, when I asked to be executed. Instead, I got "justice" by having my life be allowed to go on. I got the worst of it, so far, I'd say, because life *is* suffering. We all live under the same death sentence.

I had the same death sentence hanging over me at birth that I had when the state of Pennsylvania handed me one on paper.

Before we part, I feel there's one last bit of explaining that needs to be done.

You must know what it was that shaped me from the day I entered prison until now, what it was that I was holding onto so preciously. You need to know why I did *not* kill that guard.

You see, I made a vow to my mother to not only come home to her, but to be something worth bringing home, period. As I lay on a hospital bed following my suicide attempt in 1982, I made a vow that I was *not* going to become a monster like the people who were torturing us then. I made that vow to my mother because I was determined to show her that whatever it was that *she* went through on the outside while defending me, I would make it worthwhile, because of who I would become as a man.

It might not have seemed like much then, but, after two decades of hellish living, it finally seemed to really hold power. I did not vow revenge for those who did our family wrong. I did not vow to make everyone know my fist on their faces. What I vowed to do was much harder, because in order to hold onto anything decent about myself while on Death Row, I first had to forget what they did to me. I'll let you decide if my clinging to that vow (which I alone held onto dearly) in the face of the following litany of events that I had to endure to get to this humbling point was worthwhile.

I entered my first cell on Death Row at the age of twenty-one, only after I was "fed" to the officers by those who had just taken me roughly off of a big blue bus outside of that building.

I was stood up against the red brick wall, in a large outdoor area of the buildings inside of Huntingdon State prison in 1983. I was held there by the guards following the orders of the lieutenant on duty that day. Being "fed" to them meant that I was allowed to be beaten with their clubs and boots for thirty seconds. It was done on the order of the same lieutenant who stood among them.

That first beating was my initial payment for whatever I had actually done prior to that moment. The beating was merely to enforce the message just given to me that I was not allowed to speak while inside my cell— ever!

Afterward, I was stripped naked and tossed into cell number 447 on B-Block. I lay on the floor with my lower left incisor tooth cracked halfway down. The inside of my mouth was all ripped up from my teeth being smashed against it, as a boot ground my face into the earth. I had an egg-sized lump on my head, which was swollen at its base, which came from a blow from a metal club that was meant for my back. My nose was all caked up inside with blood from the kick to my face that I got on my way to the ground. That was before the same guy put his boot on my face and ground it into the dirt. My ribs had a series of welts on them, as did my ass cheeks, all the way down to my ankles, from where I was hit with clubs made of oak. Both legs were already turning black and blue from being clubbed. Thirty seconds is a long time for a "beat down."

Next, I was introduced to the mental anguish I would always know.

The nurse came to my cell and had fun humiliating me by instructing me how to properly fill out a prisoner sick-all slip, "should I ever need medical attention" while there. Then, she and the officer standing beside her laughed at me and ignored me, while I was standing there bleeding before them both. I did not say anything to the nurse, because the reason *that* I was beaten to begin with was to reinforce the message to me that I was not allowed to speak.

I would spend the next two years in that cell without the right to speak to anyone. On my twenty-second birthday, I became frustrated, and, in a half-hearted manner, I sang "Happy Birthday" to myself in the corner of my cell. I was then tear gassed by the guards, along with having my ass kicked good and hard. Then, medication was forcibly injected into me by a nurse while four guards held me down. It was nasty.

If you defied them and made any noise, they "extracted you" by force like that, and put you into deep seclusion while you were out of your mind on drugs. They did that by having four of the biggest human beings, wearing padded combat outfits, all line up in front of your door at once. A nurse, who was wearing a helmet and a face shield, was there behind them, and she was holding one of the biggest needles I ever saw in my life in her hands, and she was ready to stick me with it.

Inside that needle was either a drug called Thorazine, or one called Haldol (or some other psychotropic drug) that was going to fry my brain for a week. I knew it was coming, as they pulled the bar that held my door securely locked. I could feel their power, as that wave of charged-up humanity come rushing in and they pinned me down. They made sure not to beat me too much, because the nurse had to get that needle into me. So they pinned me hard while she jabbed that metal point deep into my ass.

Once the nurse stepped clear of it all, *then that is when I got the beating.*

The next bad beat-down turned me into a puppet. In 1985, I was beaten so severely for escaping from prison that it went on for four long minutes. A mere thirty seconds would have seemed like a long time, when you considered who was doing the beating.

I was shoved into a place called the "property room" on the second floor of a building just across from the windows of my Death Row unit. Inside this well-lit room were four men clad in riot gear, who were holding four-foot-long metal riot sticks. They looked like giant ants. The word "CERT," in yellow, was all I saw written above their blacked-out face shields. It was the last thing I saw before they started beating the living daylights out of me.

The room they put me in was high enough that the men on Death Row in B-Block could look out of their cells and see me, right there on a brightly lit stage. It had ten-foot-high windows that were set every six-feet-or-so apart, allowing all those guys in their cells on Death Row to see me "get some" that night.

In the end, my right cheek bone was shattered, my left retina was damaged for life, my six, upper front teeth were broken off halfway, and five of my bottom teeth were snapped off and bleeding. I had a seven-inch gash on the inside of my mouth, which had to be cauterized with a flaming-hot iron, when eighty-six stitches failed to stop the bleeding. I had cracked ribs, as well, and I learned that a lower transverse bone in my lower back was also broken that night. I pissed blood for a week.

I never have a day, ever since that beating, when I don't endure near-crippling pain because my right cheek bone re-breaks. It is deteriorating from that injury, and, at some point soon, my face will cave in. Now, I get an instant migraine whenever a prism of sunlight refracts off metal and into my left eye, anytime I go outdoors. Without the protection of the retina, that eye is unable to withstand any direct sunlight, so I will always struggle with headaches.

Mind you, all of that was done to me before I was even twenty-six years old. I then had to endure a routine for twelve years on B-Block that was aimed at breaking me mentally.

Part of that routine included a monthly effort to make me admit my guilt and to give up my appeal to be executed. Every month I had to tell them where to dispose of my body after my execution. And every month they made me defend myself for not wanting to admit how I had raped and killed Mrs. Craig, all as they sat with horrible looks on their faces when I wouldn't.

I was made to defend my being a sane human being, while they made us fight in cages, or they let men get raped in the cages, or while in the showers. Each month, they sat me down in a room and asked me to give up "my lie," face the truth, and then die. And they did all of that sick shit to others, too, year after year.

As this went on, I had to never trust any other prisoner. My neck has enough slashes to tell me that now. I had to get through so many times when, if I trusted a man, he would just sucker punch me for no reason, or try to murder me if he could. The worst of those attacks proved just as menacing as what the administration was doing to me.

The exercise cages we were made to go into daily were made of metal. Metal bends *and* rusts. There was a rod that was threaded through the whole line of fences at the bottom. That rod could be pulled up enough to be worked back and forth until a length was taken off of it. The guards searched every cell on B-Block twice a week looking for it, once they discovered that piece of fence missing. The piece of metal was twelve inches long, so they mostly wanted that shit back before it was used on one of them.

They did not find the thing because it had actually been slid into, and hidden inside, one of the pipes of the fence located about fifteen cages down from where it had been taken. It was put there after some guys passed it over to that spot the same day it was snapped off.

The guy claiming that he wanted it left outside there that day was Benjamin Porta. At that point, Ben Porta had been in prison for thirty-six years.

Who the hell was this creature from the 50s?

Ben Porta had raped and murdered a woman in Philadelphia. It was the usual "psycho sexual" murder, and the whole story is not worth wasting pages on. Ben was ruined mentally, having served thirty of his thirty-six years in solitary confinement. He was so violent that he spent *ten* years doped up and strapped to a bed. Really.

That guy laid flat on his back for a decade while inside of Rockview State Prison's mental ward! By that point, he had had drugs used on him for so many years that he was out of his mind with delirium. Always shouting and always chaotic, he was off the rails up to eighteen hours a day.

Ben also did "hits" for money. All some idiot had to do was point you out to him while telling Ol' Ben how much coin you were worth and that was it. That was what happened to me in 1990 when that wild maniac went after me with that piece of metal.

Ben got a piece of metal from the fence into the block from the tier worker. He then sat in his cell shaping it. I heard him grinding it all night on the concrete floor. I knew he was making a shank to stab someone with.

At the time, when I heard the noise of Ben making a knife, I did not know that he was making that thing to use on me. I only learned about it the next time my door opened, and he tried to use that piece of metal from the yard to stab me in my guts.

It happened when we were taken six at a time down the flight of metal stairs (that Keith had been pushed down) and moved into the shower room. The shower room was where you had your shot at guys who had no chance to defend themselves. I knew Ben was going after one of six guys in our group. Only the guy on the other side of Ben's cell and I heard him sharpening the blade. The other four guys only knew that he had a piece of metal somewhere out in the yard. I knew enough to be alert, and I tried to be on guard the next shower day.

On B-Block, a guard at the end of the cell block tier throws a long bar forward with a thud, and then six cell doors that first have had their individual locks unlatched by staff all come open at the same time. If you are at the end of the tier, right at that moment, you are able to see all six men, who have only towels around their waists, come out of their cells, their heads whipping back and forth at once. It is always the same: Look to both sides fast, then stick your head out farther.

When you do come out, always hug the side of the wall and walk so you can see the guy behind you. Do not stop, and be sure to keep your hands ready. If you can, put all your stuff in your weakest hand and be ready to punch or gouge eyeballs with your free one.

If you wear glasses, take some string and tie them on good and tight to your head. Do *not* wear socks, because they make your feet slip out of the plastic shower shoes when they are dry.

Make a hole in the corner of your towel and thread a knot onto the corner of the towel end so that it is secured like a belt to your waist. If you have to, bring a weapon, hidden inside your soap dish, or the soap bar.

As I stepped out of my cell, Ben made no attempt to play any games, however. He was an old-school gangster. He went right to his attack. He shoved the blade into my lower right side, and was pulling it out for a second plunge, when I head butted the shit out of his old ass.

He nearly went over the railing on the tier then. With my free right hand, I punched him mostly in the throat with about four good shots. Then, I used that same hand to grab the hair on his head and yanked his head backward. I was yanking hard, trying to pull him off me, as he tried to pull the blade out of me. The shank was embedded in my belly so deep that it was stuck. Ben had to let go of the blade, because my shots to his throat had him gasping badly for air.

Then, a guard hit Ben with a club to the side of his head, and he went straight down. I got popped good in the head and neck by the officer who was beside me, but I was only wobbly. Then, the guard shoved me to the floor face down.

I was screaming that I had a knife in my guts and that they were hurting me more by having me lie on my front. They were pinning me down hard with their boots, which caused all that pain in my stomach. It was only when they saw that it wasn't a ploy, that I wasn't trying to sucker punch them, and that there really was a shank in my guts from Ben's attack, that they finally let go.

When they finally let go of me, I rolled over and lay flat on my back in agony. I then pulled that thin, really dirty looking thing out of me with one hard tug. It hurt like nothing I had ever felt before. I was up on my knees, literally pissing myself after that stunt. I was curled up due to the pain, and I just could not control my bladder any longer. They took me down to the nurse's station in cuffs, and, even now, what happened next makes me sick to think about it—not so much for what they did to me, but to the person who initiated it all.

The nurse on duty needs no description. If you did time on B-Block between 1982 and 1994 (before that place was closed down) you know who I am talking about. She was in her late thirties then. She was a mean and spiteful woman who grew even worse after the 1989 riot inside Huntingdon.

I was being held down on by four officers on top of an examination bed that was set up in the "triage cell" that was on B-Block when what happened next occurred.

While each guard secured me to the examination table, the nurse took over. There was very little blood coming out of the wound, which surprised me. I was in serious pain, and my whole right side felt like it was on fire. I prayed that Ben hadn't dipped the blade in poison before he used it on me.

The nurse went into the other room, got out my file, and held it in her hands before her. Lying with my head turned toward her, as she stood in the doorway, I saw her flipping the first two pages back and forth. The first page listed the rape and murder charges for which I had been sent to death row. The second page contained escape warnings that said I was never to be dealt with "one on one by staff." As she walked from the doorway and got up close to me, she nodded to the men holding me down. Then, they each latched onto a limb and held me a little more firmly to the bed. Then it began.

"Oh look, Mr. Yarris has been hurt!" she said. "Tell me, is it bad? "Is your pain *really* bad?"

As soon as I heard her address me in that supercilious and condescending way, I shut up. I have learned that there's no point in playing the straight man to a nasty comic.

She continued. "Oh, what is that object I see sticking out of your belly, Mr. Yarris? Why, is that . . . why, yes it *is!* I think that I can see one of the fingernails belonging to Mrs. Craig sticking out of your guts!"

Then, while leaning over, she added, "She fought you *hard,* didn't she, you fucking **pig**!"

Then, as if it were a favorite treat they allowed her to have with fun with, by doing things to us "sick ones," that rotten-hearted woman stuck her finger in my belly. She fished around in the wound, where I just been stabbed, for an imaginary fingernail. I screamed and screamed until I was hoarse, as I begged her to stop. She fuckin' twisted and turned that index finger of hers, this way and that way inside of the bleeding wound. And as she did, she said, "You fucking sick piece of garbage, I hope they kill your filthy ass!"

I cried like a child, blubbering from the pain, as well as the psychotic things she said on top of it. The guards slapped me in the face, and spit in my mouth when I screamed. One guy yanked open my lips with his gloved hand, and took a whole mouthful of tobacco juice and drooled it into my mouth

I choked on their spit and twisted my head away. Then, because they all thought one last shot to my nuts was called for, they all did one round of "HOO-HA!" on my balls with their fists, and I passed out.

I was put into good old Cell 447 at the end of the block, and left there to think about how that creature of a nurse had just gotten off on her own version of "righteous justice."

I'm not done yet, though. You need to know what it was like to have that same woman greet and charm my mother, two weeks later in the visiting area room.

My mom told me that she had met the sweetest nurse ever, back then. When the nurse asked my mom, "How is Nick?" she also asked my mother if they had found the fingernail they had been looking for. When I heard that she had been toyed like that, I nearly told my mom what the fuck they had done to me.

I wanted to say things like "Mommy, please save me. Please make them stop hurting me!" I wanted to cry, and I wanted to believe that somehow God would let her take away all the shit they were doing to my head. I wanted to break down and just ball my eyes out, like I was still her little boy, all so that she could protect from bad things . . .

I cried later though, not then. I kept my shit together. I did the best that I could not to think about how fucked-up a human being had to be to play with my mother that way. Especially after they had done some of the sickest shit ever imaginable to me for no reason at all. I wiped all of that shit from my mind then, as I told my mom how I was making her a new decorated handkerchief as a gift.

I told her I was learning art designs from long ago, and how happy I was to learn that stuff. She smiled then, and I was able to keep her from catching on to what had gone down with my being stabbed. And all the while, blood was seeping from my wounds, beneath the surface of the visiting table, and well out of her sight, where she sat in the visiting booth. I stayed bent over, making sure my mom could not see what that lovely Nurse had done to her child.

Look, this has to be *it*. Even I am sick of it all and want it to be over now. I'm pouring it out while I still can. There is no point in telling you more of what I fought through, while still trying to hold onto my dignity. I need to turn off the flames on this burnt offering, so I can move on with my life.

The last thing the guard who tormented me did was open my door by himself, breaking the protocol of always having someone back him up. He said he was moving me from my cell and putting me next to Busthead. I knew right then what was up from his smiling face. He couldn't get Roland to do it, so he wanted me done in by that next guy, Busthead. I had had just about enough, so I said, "No!"

He immediately said, "Misconduct! You are getting your shit taken away for ninety days!"

I said, "Go get the lieutenant," as I closed my door by grabbing the pie hole and sliding the door shut.

As the guard left the pod and went into the hallway, I knew what was coming next. He wasn't going to get anyone else and tell them what I had just done, instead, he went and got a riot stick out of the security locker in the control booth. Then, he came back onto the pod and told me that if I did not pack up my cell belongings, he was going to shove that stick up my ass.

So I started pacing back and forth in my cell. I was torn between wanting to tell him to "kick that mother fucking door open right now, and lets get this shit on" and wanting to figure out what my best play was.

I was just walking back and forth, the anger like steam coming out of my ears. I was pumped up with rage and fear. I was at the point where I was not anywhere near rational in my thoughts. That guy was all primal and tense. I was finally going to go off on him.

The guard saw that I wasn't "passive Nick" any more, and he was sure that the stick he was holding might not be enough. Now he wasn't so sure he could handle all the rage that had been brewing inside of me. Then, he switched tactics. He told me he was coming back in five minutes, and he was putting boxes in front of my cell for me to put my belongings in. He said I better put my shit in them, and have my hands out the door to have cuffs put on them, when he got to my door upon his return.

To be safe, I wasn't putting my hands out, and I damn sure wasn't doing anything he said until I saw someone wearing bars on his shoulders, who I could talk to about that shit. Until then, I was staying in that cell, and he would have to come in and get me—one on one.

My heart felt as though it would pop from all of that shit, when I heard him coming back from the hallway. He tossed the boxes in front of my door, stepped back a step, and called out to the control booth for my cell door to be opened remotely. The door popped free of its lock then. I pushed it sideways, sliding it open fully, and I said again, "I wanna see the lieutenant."

The guard simply said, "Boxes!" I reached down with my hand to take hold of the first box. That was when he slid the metal door of my cell shut with all his might, right on top of my left hand, which was instantly crushed.

White hot pain shot up my arm, and I literally shook like I was being electrocuted.

(Even today, I have a huge mass of unhealed broken bones in my left hand from that incident. Every day, when I move my hand, a tendon "jumps" across it, causing me pain all through my fingers. That prisoner, Curry, broke most of my fingers on that same hand with his "snag," but the whole back of my hand will always be deformed from being smashed in a door frame. I can use it now okay, but it, too, has become my "Mistress Of Pain," as I call my many broken bones.)

That guard knew then, as soon as he saw my hand swelling up like a basketball, that he was screwed. That was "paperwork," right there, folks. He was going to be investigated because that was a major injury. He raised his club like he was going to go all "in for a penny, in for a pound" on my head with it. I was in so much pain that the whites of my eyes were showing. I slid down the wall onto to my knees, holding my crushed hand while ignoring him and his words. I don't know why he didn't just bash my head in and get it over with. I honestly do not.

When he left the pod, I stuck my hand in the metal toilet and flushed it over and over, to let the cold water help numb the pain.

I stayed in my cell overnight, and no one came or bothered to follow up on what he had done.

Two days later, I got called out for a visit, though, and the handcuffs would not fit my wrists because of the swelling. They called in the doctors, and then a captain of the guards got involved, too. It all blew up inside the unit, and, within hours, I was put on a special bus with heavily armed men. I was driven sixty miles south of Pittsburgh, to where Greene County super-max prison awaited me.

Sadly for me, the guard who tormented me also had a son, who worked at Greene County Prison, waiting for me. He had a message for me when I landed inside that prison, later that day. It was simple: I was to keep my mouth shut like his father told me to, or he would finish the job that his daddy had begun.

Now that I am free (and, hopefully, you, the guard who antagonized me the most, are a drunken mess in life somewhere), I hope you are reading this book and you see that we all know what a piece of work you truly are.

I healed from that guy mashing my hand to pulp, but the Hepatitis-C that I contracted back in Huntingdon when they broke my teeth (and turned my mouth into mush) was what I had to face *after* Pittsburgh.

My body began to die. I tried to fight it happening. I was put on cancer-fighting drugs that were so strong that I was made toxic by them, in order to kill the virus. It got to the point where I was temporarily blinded from being so severely over-medicated. My internal organs were also badly damaged by the medications. Overall, my life span has been shortened by what was done to me, either illness-wise or injury related. So be it.

In 2002, some seven years after I talked my friend Keith into killing himself, I, too, wrote to the courts and asked to be executed. I was saved in those final days by DNA testing results from the evidence that was once all thought to be lost. All along, they learned, I had not been some lying, crazy madman who was pulling a hoax on all the world.

My "punishment" in life for *not* being a murderous monster or a sick madman, is that everyone will always think that I was left somehow "diminished" by what I went through. I was treated like I was insane, and tortured badly while in prison.

Those were acts done *to* me, not *by* me to others.

Yet I am now suspected of being possibly insane for enduring that torture, having been innocent all along while. It is not fair, and it sucks when I have to prove myself to people because of a notion in their heads.

I have learned that the notion they have of my being somehow "off" mentally in *some* way is really nothing I can answer to. What I know to be true is that I bet no one else could have handled what I have and still be as level-headed as I am.

So, that brings me back to what I pointed out earlier: I went through all the mentally cruel stuff I did with only one intention: I was going to keep my vow to Jayne Yarris, my mother, as I promised her I would.

I was going to make sure that their torturing only resulted in good. How can I ever explain how I put aside my own battle to preserve my sanity, all so that I could make every effort as a man to keep my simple promise to my mother?

I would make sure that whoever put her down on the outside, saw, later on, that I was a nice man when I got out for that very reason. That way, everyone could see why my mother had stuck by me through all those years. I was going to ignore all that was done to me in a prison cell, because of one thing that I know to be true. It is one truth that many will never know actually:

"Freedom" is some made-up bullshit.

You are a prisoner to every person whom you ever loved or cared about in life. You are a prisoner to life itself, and a prisoner to all whom you care for, or want inside your life. As such, don't be a punk-ass "inmate."

Do not become complacent and take the easy way, while you let yourself just be a suck-up to everyone around you. Don't try to hold onto the notion of acting like a "convict," whereby you live by some code that has you going around acting dominant over others.

No, be like Lonnie. Be a good "prisoner." Don't listen to what the "social world" around you says you must do in order to have an opinion. Pay attention to what determines how you treat people face-to-face. Deal with them as fairly as they deserve, based upon the respect that they give to you.

The people in your world may not like how you do that at times, but, at least, they will have to respect you for being honest to their face. Be consistent. Just be yourself in that way.

I wrote this book for a reason. When I met Laura and we fell in love, I told her then that I had this "thing" within me that I had to finally let go of. SHE was the one who asked me why I did not just write it all down in a book. So I did. I wrote this book in three days, with her watching over me, while she fed me and cared for me. She stood guard over each tear that I shed until I was free of it all at last.

If you are disappointed that there is no more material for you to read, I cannot help that. I am a storyteller, and *this* story is clearly over. I think I have shared one of my best stories with you—one of how I learned of myself once again. It has to stop now, though, because there are no big points left to make. I finally got out of that unit, after being maimed, and yet I killed no one, in spite of all my suffering.

I love that I finally had enough good things happen to me in my life as a free man, that I was able to write this wonderful work at this time in my life. The fact that I ended up writing it all here in Somerset England, on this pretty April Day in 2016, is so very representational of what I hold myself to be as a man. It's important to be able to accept when you need others in order to grow.

Thank you Laura Ann Yarris. I proudly have your name tattooed on my flesh, while you also wear mine proudly as your own. Thank you for helping me get this story out in a way that doesn't take away from my overall message of how I developed while in prison. That was such a fear of mine that you helped me with, Babe. You made me understand that it doesn't matter if I share this tale, because it shows that I was a loving man despite my bad days. I know you will love me through all of my days, whether they are good or bad, because you know I will remain the same inside.

The end of this work was the beginning of my time with my wife, Laura, and our children in 2016. I like that. I took that shittiest walk in life back then inside of prison, only to hold on long enough to now walk in the elegance of love — all without being owned one bit by anger from it all.

The End

Postscript

I want to say one last thing, as best I can, about this book:

Man, I cannot believe I *made* it. I did it. I got through it all, and by telling about it, I have somehow completed my writing about prison. I need not bother with any more prison books now, as all of the ghosts of my past are now sheets that are hanging on laundry lines. It's all sweetly over . . .

Bye and thank you. I love you for reading this book of mine and, no, you are not "sick" or "wrong" for laughing your ass off at a guy with a pen sticking out of his asshole . . . it's allowed.

With love always,

Nick

About the Author

Nick Yarris was born in Philadelphia in May of 1961. Before him came three older sisters and an older brother, Michael, then, afterward, his younger brother, Martin.

Both brothers are now dead, as is his mother, as well. His father still resides in Southwest Philly. This is Nick's fourth published book. The others are: *The Fear of 13*, *The Kindness Approach*, and *Seven Days to Live: This is My Story*.

"I am harder than life, yet kinder than love."
That's my motto.

If you understand this notion about yourself, then everything that I have tried to share here is worth it to me, because it means that *you* are sharing that same feeling in life.

Nick

Printed in Great Britain
by Amazon

27068853R00138